JOURNEY
An Anthology

Westerly Writing Group
2019 edition

ISBN: 978-1-7339346-2-6

Book design by Gigie Hall

CONTENTS

WRITING IS FOR EVERYONE

When I first asked the director of the library if I could start a writing group, I had, more or less, no real clue what I was doing. But the magic of a group is that you're not in it alone; everyone has a piece, place, and power in shaping our direction. I knew I wanted to write, wanted to do it with others who had important stories to tell, and wanted, maybe, to stir up a little unrest. A little fire. All the rest was the journey.

Something that's always mattered to me with this group, and working in the library's teen space at the time, is that everyone feels the right to call themselves a writer. That journey doesn't start once you've had a book reviewed and approved by the right people, or stamped "literary" by the right publishers and critics. Nor is it really about how smart you sound, how delicate your craft, or how eloquent your rhetoric.

Writing is for everyone.

Maybe you haven't written in forty years; perhaps you only have some scribblings in a notebook; or maybe you've dismissed yourself for so long ("I'm a bad writer!") that you can't finish more than a few sentences without erasing them. Most of us have roadblocks to believing we have a story worth telling, and usually, they aren't ones we've created. They're ones we've learned through pain, rejection, or misunderstanding.

We regulars have seen it a number of times now. Someone shows up, a bit nervous, and more than a little reluctant to share. They make a few self-deprecating remarks. Wave off the request to read what they've written. "Oh, I don't know…" they mutter. "I don't want to be a downer." Or, "this really isn't any good." But we're a persistent bunch! So, after much encouragement (see also: nagging), they begin to read. Maybe with a shaky voice. Maybe with some tears. Maybe for the first time. Out loud. But they read.

A writing group doesn't just give you feedback on your craft or suggestions on how to improve your syntax. A writing group gives you radical permission to be yourself—whoever you are—and to say what you must say without fear of judgment. More than anything, you all have showed me what a powerful force that can be.

Despite what anyone is made to think, there are people who want to hear you. They want to hear the stories you've struggled to tell. They want to understand the journey you've walked. They want to learn what you've learned and feel what you've felt. They want, in short, to know you!

And we're often closer than you might imagine. Maybe even at your local library.

— Erik Caswell

Part 1

BEGINNINGS

SUNRISE
Al Clemence

In the darkness of early morning, when sleep no longer binds me to my bed, I rise to seek a place to sit and rest my still weary head. I find my way through rooms with light that would not suffice when weariness bade me pass the other way.

A chair by a window in a quiet room is where I pause. It is not by chance that I have chosen this special place. With my head resting on the cushion, I become a compass that points to that northern star that never moves. Lifting my eyes, I search for a place in the still dark sky that marks the line around the Sun where I reside.

As the moments pass, I sense the movement of the Earth as it turns to face the dawn. There are other wanderers that share my path, respecting the summons of the Sun. Flashes like fireflies appear without notice, then disappear without warning. Some heralded by pageantry, appear to pull a shroud of the whitest silk across the sky. Travelers, seemingly exempt from the forces that guide my path, destined for places I will never see. I watch as the sun draws the curtain on the night, then responding to energy that cannot be ignored, I begin the duties of the day.

WHEN DOES HUMAN LIFE BEGIN?
Hugh M. Ryan

Both science and religion address the question at hand, which I am limiting for my essay to when human life begins. This raises a corollary question: when does life as a human begin? In other words, when are we dealing with a living organism with the potential to be a human being and when do we encounter a fully developed human herself?

My essay sets aside religion's answers because they emanate from faith and so are not open to scientific inquiry or rational proof. I do not dismiss religious belief or believers, but in this inquiry, choose to examine what science, not religion, tells us about the origin of human life.

Scientific research in anatomy, genetics, and physiology continuously reveals more and more about human life and its origin. Science's simple answer to the beginning of human life is fertilization of an egg by a sperm cell. At that point, a living organism exists that, after approximately nine months' gestation, may become an infant. That is different from saying that, scientifically, it is a human being. Two weeks after fertilization, the blastocyst, whose inner cells will form the embryo, is the size of a poppy seed.[1] It has none of the limbs, organs, functions, or capabilities of a human.

At this point, the blob of cells that will become a baby starts to form into organs and tissue. Chromosomes, threadlike structures of nucleic acids and protein found in the nucleus of most living cells, carry genetic information and instructions in the form of genes.[2] Nerve cells, blood cells, cells that will become the lining of the intestine, and all other constituents of a human body begin to form.

At four-and-a-half weeks from fertilization, an embryo has grown to a fifth of an inch; parts of its brain, other organs, and limbs are forming. At four months, the embryo, now a fetus, is one inch long, weighing a third of an ounce. Its organs are in place, but not functioning. By the ninth week,

---

[1] "The Greatest Miracle," *Nova*, PBS-TV, available on YouTube. This program provided the bulk of the science in this essay.
[2] Merriam-Webster.com

the retinas and lenses have formed in the eyes, but the fetus does not respond to light until the fifth or sixth month. The timing is approximately the same for the development of the ear and the fetus's response to sound. Other organs begin to function.

In the final trimester of pregnancy, myelin, an insulating layer or sheath, forms around nerves, crucially including those in the brain and spinal cord to allow electrical impulses to transmit quickly and efficiently along the nerve cells.[3] Hence, human brain activity.

So, what does science tell us about when life as a human begins? As a non-scientist, I approach this question with humility, acknowledging my ignorance, and determined to listen to the scientists without prejudgment.

My understanding of the science of human life, its origin and its starting point, is that life as a human begins months after conception, but before the moment of birth, in the third trimester of pregnancy. At that point, my reading of science is that we are dealing no longer with a fetus, but with a baby, entitled to life, liberty, and the pursuit of happiness, which is where pollsters tell us the majority of Americans instinctively stand.

---

[3] *QBP Science Encyclopedia*, New York: Helicon Publishing Group, 1999, p. 508.

ONSET
Eric Maynard

One oval, gaseous, and molten, a celestial body
with terrestrial pores, elliptical primordial pools
breathing, tides, undertows
Woven coats, folds of skin stretching, cracking,
more ovals from more ovals, pulsing, pumping, shifting, shimmering
Incipient streams surging, surrounding, ovate, inchoate
Tectonic plates push and grind, a dance,
a flash,
a BANG,
fatigue cracking
more ovals inside of ovals, more ruptures, more fission
New canyons, new mountains, new cobblestone
more ovals, more eggs, more churning and buzzing
Hives, hordes multiplying, brood propagating
more ovals, the landscape,
the life-scape
the brain-scape,
A thought, a birth of passion from mind-seed to engineered calisthenics
Labor,
keystrokes,
bearing down,
bearing fruit,
Eggplant, papaya, apricot,
Delivery.

Part 2

CHILDHOOD DAYS

FLEEING

Katherine Marotta

In my dream he is fleeing
trying to get somewhere
but mostly trying to run free
away from harm's way
which seems to be another human

there is fear
there is urgency
running and glancing for brief seconds
over his left shoulder

I am there to assist
but I am also running
having difficulty keeping the pace needed
to avoid being caught too

caught to suffer
into someone's intense desire
to catch him and hurt him
stop him from running free

I assist by being with him
and he appreciates my assistance
we never get caught in this dream
but we leave the dream while we are running

KINDERGARTEN
Katherine Marotta

School, my haven of self-worth
Entering first with trepidation, maybe? I don't recall
Watching and listening for directions
Experiencing...loving it all.

Painting and playing, songs, snacks, slides, and swings
Feeling all of those things...
All mine and school was divine.

At snack time one day, I had a doughnut, a half
My friend, a boy, Albert, my buddy, sat near
He wanted some, of that doughnut, it was clear.

Sure, but how to share it I did not know,
I unwrapped the wax paper, sugar all on it, ready to go.

The jelly on my finger for me to enjoy
Was sucked off so quickly by that little boy
My finger got wet and my stomach upset
A moment of horror I can never forget.

Wearing a pretty dress and patent leather shoes
At Kindergarten graduation I sang a solo which I did not want to do
Where is "thumb-kin" anyway? Hiding with my terror
I did it, no error, knowing singing it again I would never.

So young I discovered a performer I'm not
That pleasure forever
Repressed when asked to be a "little teapot."

School house stories, there are many to tell
Yet every school day did not always go well

My kindergarten classmate, Little Johnny Krauther seemed angry and frightened
Making kindergarten memories exceedingly heightened.

He'd go hide in the closet and make so much noise
Mrs. Birdsole said he was not allowed to play with the toys
Ignore him, we were told, and we tried, impossible to do
He would scream and pound and then throw his shoe.

Everyone knowing Johnny was not like all the rest
Because he was scary being more than a pest
One day in his teens he was to be found
Hanging from a tree in our woods...lost
I hold the memory of his sound

SCHOOL DAYS
Mel Jolly

I often have wondered not only what makes a good teacher, but also how to discern if a person is a great teacher. I raise this question because years ago, actually 1950, in Muncie, Indiana, I was faced with a situation which puts this question to the test.

When I was in the third grade at Washington Elementary School, I was the only minority student in my class. My teacher announced that the school had decided to stage a patriotic tribute to some of history's great Americans and then further explained that our class would audition for the role of our First President, George Washington. Recognizing that she really was addressing only the boys in the class, we all responded with typical childhood enthusiasm. One by one, our teacher called all the boys to the front of the room, where each donned a white powdered wig and then read a card saying, "Yes Father, I cannot tell a lie, I chopped down the cherry tree."

In time, silence overcame the room, but I realized our teacher had not called my name. I raised my hand and as she acknowledged me, I said, "You didn't call my name!" Our teacher admitted that she had not and invited me to come forward. At the front of the room with my back to the class, I reached for the card, but our teacher reminded me that I had forgotten to put on the wig. Still with my back to the classroom, I picked up the wig, positioned it on my head, and then once again reached for the card. I turned to face my classmates but as I started to read, I began to hear giggles and snickers. The giggling quickly turned to chuckling, until finally it became outright uncontrollable laughter. Somehow, the image of a black boy being relatable to President Washington was incomprehensible to the young minds of my classmates. In retrospect though, that reaction simply was the mindset cultivated by the American socialization of the era.

Now, as I reflect upon that scene of so long ago, the question becomes clear. Did my teacher have the foresight to know what would happen and therefore deliberately skip me? In reality, was she protecting her young black student from being taunted, or did she truly feel that presenting a black child as a president was in fact ridiculous? Was she a good teacher because she was sensitive towards the situation, or was she a poor teacher because she was insensitive toward a black student?

I would like to think my teacher understood the ramifications and consequences that would be faced by the young black student in her charge. Equally though, I am confident she realized that this child would be both ill-equipped and unprepared to fight back against discrimination and prejudice at such an early age. Perhaps she even was aware that strengthening of the soul, or thickening of the proverbial skin, would be needed, yet was a long way off in the developmental process. Within this scenario, I reflect upon my teacher as being a good teacher, but was she a great teacher?

Today, as I think back upon my teacher and my young classmates, I realize that this sequence of events in my third grade classroom could have been a golden opportunity for a teaching moment. A great teacher might have been able to turn the situation into a meaningful learning experience, an opportunity to help impressionable young minds understand compassion. Hopefully in today's world, nearly 70 years later, that would be the approach—and the difference that might distinguish a good teacher from a great teacher.

Part 3

A NOVEL IN PROGRESS

An Excerpt from

MISDEMEANOR MURDERS
Andy Rosenzweig

Salvatore Lisi is right out of central casting. Though he's pushing fifty and has been abusing drugs his entire adolescent and adult life, he's somehow managed to maintain a youthful appearance—partially due to the way he dresses. Sal's a fashionista! Whatever the current styles are he's there, getting his clothes from one of several thrift shops.

He's also a small man, barely over five feet tall and he weighs about a 105. He had thoughts of being a jockey when he was a teenager but had never been atop a horse, so that was sheer fantasy. It didn't keep him from the racetracks though. His favorite, Narragansett, is in what they call South County in that part of Rhode Island. There was a certain intimacy there—everyone seemed to know each other.

Sal is comfortable getting close to groups of people involved in intimate or confidential conversations, knowing to keep his mouth shut and to communicate mostly with a smile or facial expression. Quickly, he was accepted around the track as just one more "character."

Same with the drug scene in New Netherland. Sal has been around for so long that he rarely gets questioned. And if he does, he has an act.

"Who the fuck are you to ask me that! No really, who the fuck are you motherfucker! I'll break your fucking ass you ask me that again, you hear?"

It would go like that for a few minutes and usually the other person became amused at "the midget's" aggressiveness. That's how he was often referred to on the street: "You seen the midget, where the fuck's the midget, that fucking midget's a piece of work!"

So for over twenty-five years, Sal Lisi fooled them all. It helps tremendously that his one rule is inviolate—he'll never testify in a case. There might be hints or rumors or suspicions from time to time, but the fact that Sal never set foot in a courtroom to raise his right hand supported his effectiveness as a snitch.

Enter Sydney Jackson. She wants him to testify. To go into a grand jury and testify about what he knows about the victims of the triple murder.

"No fucking way baby. Never gonna happen. You can lock me up, beat me up, do whatever—you're never getting me into that building."

"Sal, it's a grand jury, a secret proceeding. No one's gonna know."

"Syd, sweetie. You gotta be shitting me. There's what, twenty-five grand jurors? And the judge, and the clerk, and the bailiff. And this is freaking New Netherland—very few secrets here, babe. Maybe the last one is me— that I'm a mother fucking rat! You know what happens I get outed?"

"Sal...."

"No, seriously, you know what happens? The old man hears about it and he gets a couple of gindaloons off Federal Hill to grab me off the street. They drive me forty-five minutes up to Providence, to one of the junk yards near Fox Point, get me way back near the river and they torture my sorry ass. Cut my tongue out for starters, to send a clear message, then they do a number on my privates. Then if these jabonies got an ounce of humanity in them, they'll put me out of my misery. More likely they'll let me lay there in the mud a few hours, screaming, but I won't be able to scream much because I got no fucking tongue by that point, see. Then...."

"Okay, Sal, enough, you made your point. I had to ask though."

"You had to ask, you had to ask. I tell you Syd, you got my blood pressure through the roof, here. Least you could do—give me a blow job."

Sal laughs when Sydney Jackson slaps him, says, "You need a sense of humor detective. You got a long way to go before you collect your pension."

Sydney Jackson stuffs a ten-dollar bill in Sal's shirt pocket then leans across and opens the passenger door of her unmarked police cruiser and gives Sal a small shove. When he gets out on the unpaved trail at Sachuest Point, the wildlife sanctuary at the eastern end of New Netherland, he protests, saying how the fucks he going to get back to the city.

"Fresh air will do you good dipshit."

Sydney glances in her rearview mirror and cracks a smile when she sees Sal kicking the dirt. She drives into the center of the city to police headquarters. When she enters the garage, the light-duty officer gives her a wave. They know each other from the Academy and from their first days walking a beat in the Fifth Ward. *Good cop, Tom Lalli*, she thinks to herself. Only trouble was, he let his enthusiasm get the best of him. She remembers the night he got shot, on the roof of a six-story walkup. The call had come over—"man with a gun"—and they both got to the building at the same time. They had adjoining foot posts and when they converged at the entrance to 111 Thames Street, they encountered a hysterical woman whose words ran together in indecipherable confusion. She pointed to the roof, saying he had a gun. Sydney implored Tommy to wait for backup but he was gone in an instant. Sydney remained with the woman. The gunshot wound to his lower abdomen would never quite heal correctly, even though he spent six weeks in New Netherland General with the best medical care.

"How'd you make out with the midget?" Buster asks.

"Okay, he'll nose around, see if he can get anything."

"Good, the guy has a way of coming up with solid tips from time to time."

"You gonna buy me dinner, Lieutenant?"

He's stunned by the question. Till this moment, he thought they were done. He's been looking for a place he can afford, not wanting to stay any longer than necessary in the HQ dorm. People are starting to notice, starting to talk. Now he wonders—is there a chance?

They have an early dinner at Forlini's, on Market Street, by the commercial fishing piers in lower Newport. It's one of the few streets that still uses the name of the old city by the sea. It's a period piece of a building, three stories of red brick and dark green casement windows, the first two devoted to the restaurant, the top floor an office, and a second room that serves as an occasional flop for the owners or friends of theirs.

"Calamari's sweet, melt in your mouth," she says.

"They've got the secret down. Never had a bad dish here."

"We gonna break this case, Buster?"

"Of course we're gonna break it. Triple murder…we better solve it."

Her smile almost lights up the room. Her teeth are radiant white and set against her black skin, it's even more illuminating. She wears a medium red lipstick. Her brown silk blouse and tan pantsuit top pull at her chest. When she invites him to come over he can barely conceal his enthusiasm. So much so that he comes close to dissing his good friend Freddy Forlini.

"What's the rush? Stop at the bar, Dempsey give you some Sambuca, on the house."

The raconteur Tony Bennett doppelganger is nothing if not charming. But Buster Crowley gives him a quick smile and a pat on the back as they walk out the door. Freddy gives him a knowing wink.

The next morning he wakes up to the smell of brewing coffee. But he's not sure where he is. He panics for a minute, sitting bolt upright, thinking about his gun. Where's my gun? When she walks in with two steaming mugs of coffee he finally relaxes.

"You feel okay baby?" she says.

"Yes, feel okay…much better than that."

He snaps back to thinking about the murders of the three boys. *That's all they are, boys*, he thinks to himself, *and I don't give a shit if they're selling drugs, that's still some momma's little boys.*

Detective Sylvester O' Hara laughs at Lieutenant Buster Crowley when he repeats his thoughts about the victims, that they have mothers who are grieving. Ordinarily, a detective doesn't laugh in the face of his boss, but when you're the bagman for the city's biggest and most corrupt power broker and he's the brother of your boss, well, let's say it gives O'Hara some special leeway.

"How's my brother doing, Syd?"

"Big Jim? Oh he's grand lieutenant, just grand."

At least I got him to quit calling be Declan, Buster Crowley thinks. Then he realizes he smells whiskey on O'Hara's breath. He stares at him and notices a red stain on his pale blue shirt and a splatter on his striped blue and white tie. *What a bum, what a freaking disgrace. What choice do I have though? I got to carry the son-of-a-bitch.*

Part 4

A STORY BY THREE WRITERS

HE SHOULD NEVER HAVE PINCHED HIS CHEEK

Andy Rosenzweig, Eric Maynard, and Wendy Bradford

I'm a bit player in all this but I was there for most of it. It's about three tough guys, all good with their hands. Two of them, Richie Gannon and Jimmy Morton, are professional fighters who outmatch the average Joe, but the third guy, Frankie Kunstler, he's got his own advantage—he'll shoot you in a heartbeat and everyone down at the docks in New Netherland knows that.

Me, I'm no fighter, more of a lover I like to say. But anyone gives me too hard a time, I got a thirty-four ounce Louisville slugger stashed behind the stick. I bartend four nights a week, at Mickey Dunn's joint, next-door to Vinnie Paz's gym. It's not really Vinnie Paz's though—he let two guys from up Federal Hill use his name and they give him so much a week for the privilege.

Mickey's is a real bucket of blood, especially on weekends. Mick stays with me till closing, so between the two of us there's not too much we can't handle—except for guys like Kunstler. We're wary of that son-of-a-bitch, keep him at arm's length. But nice, nice—make sure he gets his buybacks.

Jimmy and Richie? They got their own issues.

Jimmy's a welterweight, has over forty fights under his belt, and a face that looks it. He's fought a few contenders and only lost half a dozen times, so he's no slouch. He's got the look of someone who works the docks or construction: wears worn tan construction boots and faded jeans, and navy sweatshirts with the sleeves cut off.

Richie though, is Mr. Fashion Plate in sharp looking suits, long sleeved shirts buttoned to the top, with shined shoes he gets buffed every day down the Amtrak terminal. And his hair's black and long, with a pompadour that he likes to give a little flourish to. Some guys say that maybe he's a switch-hitter, but that would surprise me, because every other time he walks in he's got a different bottle blond floozy on his arm. And as a fighter he's also no slouch, with maybe twenty bouts (but he's lost half of them).

Two weeks ago Mick gets the bright idea that we need a couple of bouncers for the weekend and asks the two palookas do they want the job? They jump at the chance when he offers three bills each for a six-hour night. Don't you know things go bad the first night? You see Mick is a pushover as a boss, likes to be friends with everyone. So when Richie Gannon says, *can we have a couple of drinks*, he says *sure*. And Richie, Mr. big mouth, orders two Grey Gooses neat, for him and his pal. When I hand them to him with about an inch of vodka he gives me the fish eye.

"Problem, Richie?"

"Short pour, Vic…don't be such a Jew."

Right away he starts with the wise cracks, and that's without having a taste. Then he shoves the two glasses back at me, so what am I gonna do? I fill 'em half way up and give them back. He's not gone ten minutes when he comes back for more. That's when I know this is gonna be a long night.

The place is filling up, mostly with dockworkers, and a few other fighters from the gym, and some nurses and secretaries like the atmosphere. Joe Cocker's singing from the juke—*give me a ticket for an airplane*—and the smokes so thick I'm probably gonna have emphysema or worse before long. And who walks in? Last guy I wanna see, that's who.

"How you, Frankie?"

"Doing good, Vic. How bout you?"

"Couldn't be better…what are you having?"

"Makers, rocks. Where's Mick?"

I direct him back of the pool table, close to the jukebox. He walks back with his drink, says hello to Mick. I see them shake hands, then see Frankie give a nod to Richie and Jimmy. They turn their backs on him. I'm busy behind the stick, can't wait for the second bartender to get there, but I look up at the three of them and now they're nose to nose in some sort of tête-à-tête. Next thing I see blows me away. Richie Gannon reaches up and pinches Kunstler's cheek. And I think to myself, is he crazy? Why'd he do that?

Richie twisted the pinch around Kunstler's apple red face flesh with a sadistic smirk. Kunstler gritted his teeth, balling up his right hand around Richie's grip, and tossing it off his cheek like he's swatting away a pesky gnat. From behind the bar and over the sound of the juke and the nurses and boxers and whatnot, I couldn't hear any of Richie's and Kunstler's back-and-forth. I'm no trained lip reader or nothin' but between pours of Dewars and Pavlov, I see Kunstler call Richie a "mother" something, and Richie respond with two words, one beginning with "f" and the other ending with "u."

Damn it, I think. These dumb bastards are getting into it right here and now.

I had a few seconds to piece together what I was going to do about it. I look around, and Mick's nowhere to be found. He's the one that should be keeping his new employees in line, not me. Who the hell am I?

Then Richie makes a bigger mistake. He grabs Kunstler by his collar, and pulls him forward, his other hand a fist, shaking, pulsing close to Kunstler's twitching enraged eyes. Kunstler, who I can suddenly hear as Joe Cocker ends, calls Richie a "god damned dandy." *Dandy,* I say to myself. *What the f's a dandy?*

It all happens so fast. Kunstler rears up and lands a punch on the left side of Richie's face. Richie takes it, and lands an uppercut on Kunstler's chin. Jimmy, who unlike Richie isn't wearing a suit he's afraid of getting wrinkled, grabs Kunstler by the hair as Richie takes another swing at him.

I reach down to find the only "human resources" tool in the joint—my Slugger.

Then I think, what the hell am I going to do to these three heavy hitters? Christ, if I'm pulling this bat out I better be prepared to knock all three of them out. And then I gotta serve booze to them later tonight or tomorrow? And Richie and Jimmy might still keep their jobs and I gotta stare at their dumb mugs for god knows how long….

And then a bigger worry worms its way into my head: what if Kunstler's packing heat and decides to use it? Beer steins and bottles shattered, tables overturned, Kunstler elbowing Jimmy and getting him to let go of his hair.

As I stand there, I suspect that someone is gonna get shot. I says to myself, *Mick, why the hell did you play nice with these oversize babies and give 'em jobs protecting the bar when the bar needs protecting from them?*

"Mick!" I holler.

No Mick. I have to stop thinking and act. I'm not sure how I'm going to do it, but I excuse myself from the dockworker front of me looking for a belt, and hop the stick Slugger in hand.

"Mick! Mick, get yer ass out here now!"

Just then he comes out from the back room. I can see on his face he's stunned by what he's seeing. He starts walking over to the swinging hambones, hands extended, palms out saying, "Hey, hey…hey, c'mon fellas…c'mon…."

That's when Mick takes one on the chin himself. It's a freaking donnybrook and I can't tell who tagged him.

Mick teeters. I can't see his face but time, men, and place seem suspended. *Shit,* I say to myself, looking at my slugger. I need a big diversion or these motherfuckers will wreck the whole place. Much as I don't like to admit it, I like the job and don't want to lose it because of a testosterone brawl. But if

Kunstler's packing, I've got bigger worries. Someone might end up dead. I turn back towards the bar and see three of the nurses huddled together in the corner. Three sets of eyes wide open watching the impromptu boxing match. Millie, nice broad I've known a while, shrugs her shoulders.

"Guys, always trying to compare who's the longest," she says.

"Ladies, if you can turn that boxing match into a cocktail party, you got free drinks for two weeks."

"You're gonna take care of us?"

The babe named Virginia rests her hand on my shoulder. I know she has something for me but now is not the time.

Hanna, the third barfly, glides off the bar stool, checking her cleavage and straightening her uniform.

"Follow me, ladies. Let's get this done."

I happily watch every sinuous step as each picks one of the brawlers and leans against him. Virginia goes right up to Kunstler.

"Frankie, I'm bored…let's dance sweetie?"

The other two take Richie's and Jimmy's hands and begin to dance to Clapton's "You Look Wonderful Tonight."

Mickey, now among the living, turns and walks back to the bar.

"I was sure he was going to pull out his piece. What ya do?"

"Nothing much. Just promised the girls free drinks for two weeks."

"What?"

"Small price for your stupidity, Mick. Everyone knows Frankie's always packing. You're damn lucky someone wasn't hurt. And I still don't get you hiring Richie and Jimmy as bouncers."

As I watch Virginia dancing with Frankie, I wonder if I'll ever get close to her again. His arm has a firm grip on her back. It just might be too high a price to pay. Guess I'll get my line back in the water, look to land another one.

Part 5

THE ENVIRONMENT

SOMETHING STRANGE ABOUT
THE WATERS
Erik Caswell

They think I do not remember, but I do. Even with my cloudy eye, and through the murky stench of this river, I remember.

There was a time this land was named for us, for the relationship we had with its inhabitants, whose tongues were shaped by and more sensitive to the shallow, slow moving muddy waters we call home. Misquamicut. Most of them do not remember now, what it even means. Or that in pursuit of their vacations, their restaurants, their decadence they confuse for happiness, they have indeed turned this into something other than "land of the red fish." The word but a shallow droll uttered by the mechanized voice of a GPS. Nothing of its original invocation remains. And salmon has become merely a color palette for their canvas shorts.

Immediately, we noticed the change. Pale hungry faces peeking through the tiny chopping motion of river waves. But it did not matter much at first. Even as they spread on either shore year to year, while the faces we'd grown familiar with, grown to love, had gone off—exiled. When their numbers were few, we'd considered them merely the latest land dwellers.

But their hunger is insatiable. That is all we know. That hunger has pushed us to the verge of extermination. It's as though they fish to eat for several hundred thousand. It is as though they could eat every last one of us and still, somehow, hunger.

Our life was already hard. Intermediaries, we are. Beings of the sea and river. Each year we travel upstream from the ocean, fins flailing against the current that cannot keep us from tomorrow, seeking a soft, slow place to lay our eggs. It is a noble journey, to bring children into the world who can survive and contribute to it. We salmon are not too dense to recognize it.

But with the machines, the water wheels, the smokestacks, the spill off, the oil rigs, and the motorized fishing boats, came the dams as well. Our breeding routes were blocked off. The eggs would wash away. They would be eaten. Smashed against sea rocks. And the fishers continued. Ceaselessly. I am but one of few in the wild who remain. They have begun to farm us now, to breed us in captivity, where we have never lived and do not belong. It's like this with them—they want the spoils of everything without sacrificing anything.

And yet, there is something strange about the waters as of late. I'm beginning to think it's catching up with them. All the smoke. All the death. The waters are irritated. They swell and sputter; the currents out at sea have altered; the sea creeps up into their yacht clubs, their summer homes, their precious beach patios. It seems they may soon meet a hunger even they cannot conceive of. And when those wild of us return, nestling in the ruins of their dams and factories, their seaside manors and the vestiges of their excesses, to once again lay our eggs, we will begin, just as its name signifies, to inhabit this land of the red fish.

They think we do not remember this, but we do. Even more keenly than they. For we have already suffered the losses they soon will have to face.

FROM POLYESTER TO PASHMINA:
A JOURNEY OF CONSCIOUS AWARENESS
Cynthia F. Davidson

It's easy to laugh at those still clad in pastel polyester but I can remember being one of them. How did I make the transition from those all too practical synthetics to the finely spun cashmere of Kashmir, the product of a *Changthangi* goat in Tibet or the northern Himalayas of India?

We can also poke fun at those white women of a certain age who do yoga, like me. In the West we have affected this drapery of damsels from the darker skinned continent where such exquisite shawls are often woven, in smoky huts at heart stopping elevations.

Once we discover the blessings of natural fibers, so light and soft, we move on from what made us itch and sweat but didn't require ironing. I can recall the drip-dry craze of convenience. How else would I have been able to travel the world for my work? Washing my own clothing in a hotel sink or a hostel kept me from being dependent upon dry cleaners who cost too much and take too long. Their process is also poisonous, as I've since learned. The solvent tetrachloroethylene PCE is a human carcinogen.

Who else weaves these worlds together but the travellers? The products of the mountain goats have clambered onto my shoulders. What travels do their herders dream of—escaping to an America glimpsed in movies while we westerners dream of escaping to a cabin in the woods? Why do I assume this? Perhaps the herders are perfectly content where they are, culling the three to six ounces of fibers shed each spring by their four leggeds, who must be combed—not sheared—to surrender their bounteous undercoats.

Meanwhile in Europe and the Americas, we are learning how many hundreds of thousands of acrylic and polyester fibers are released into the environment by each load of laundry spun through our washing machines. This adds precipitously to the microplastics whose pollution is now evident in our food chain and even our breast tumors.

Polyester is a synthetic petroleum-based fiber fashioned from a non-renewable carbon-intensive resource. Wikipedia tells us nearly 70 million barrels of oil are used each year to spin the world's polyester. Those threads take over 200 years to decompose.

And the goat's hair, what happens to that? As I wrap myself in this pashmina, I think of the woman who mailed it to me from California where her mother has just died of cancer. To raise money, she is selling off the stock of pashminas once purchased for her store. She gave us a good deal. Yet her husband also died of cancer in his 60s. All of this forces me to rethink good deals, convenience, and our global interconnectedness. Whether we want to ponder it or not, perhaps our grandchildren who survive on this planet, will rue the day polyester, plastic, and petroleum were put to such deadly use.

EMILY PETERSON'S INDEX DIGIT
Peggy Conti

who will rummage through
the hammered findings
and reattach Emily's severed finger

who will remind foreman Eddie Joe
of the request he couched to purchase
a safeguard for that damn foot press

ORINOCO
Emma Weiss

Some bend in the Orinoco might explain
How it came to be.
A man in a squat
next to an old fire dying out
making the sound of the
"O" twitching a braided vine through the embers
and pondering the sounds of rivers.

Then small granddaughter
moving high on swift little legs that take her careening down
a jungled dirt path through deep green fronds
that beat her legs
and make her weep with joy.
They carry her to a place where her grandfather burned ashes
that powder her feet as she moves swiftly
across the rocks
leaving in her wake
the thronging birds that pretend she isn't there
and footprints that coat the silted riverbed
with her.
All the while yelling "RI" as she runs unfaltering.

"No" can be heard
Just as it sounds outside the jungle too.
Hard on the roof of the mouth.
"N"
Clear as the anger that grips wrists and won't let go.
No.
Silent as the feather that floats from the air of the canopy
slow and dense with heat
dappling in a green light of sun and choices.

As careful as
"CO"
sounds soft in the back of the throat
and in its falling it will finally find its resting place
when the name for a place is found
in the dark cool earth under lianas.
Beneath a fern struck by the sound of the
Orinoco
Flowing by.

ZEKA
Katherine Marotta

I took a walk on a Brazilian coffee farm
With a dog
Who only understood Portuguese
I preferred being alone after a month of apartment living
But Zeka pushed his nose through the gate
And led me to the left...Zeka continued leading

The path or road, was dust with miles of trees to the left and right
Full of green coffee beans
My walk became our walk and the eldest dog, Luna, soon joined us

All was slow and easy, quiet, no language needed
Zeka sniffed
I absorbed the bird calls and blue above,
We stumbled over gnarled roots of unknown trees

Suddenly I spoke to Zeka as Luna limped behind
No matter if English was not his preferred language
I chatted with some desperation, no separation
Knowing Zeka was my listening companion and
the hero of my day

PASSION
Wendy Bradford

A soft breeze rustles through the leaves that dress the trees surrounding me. I sit on my deck reading, cloaked in a natural cocoon of ease. At the northwest corner, a baker's rack displays five differently shaped pots in bright colors filled with blossoms, cascading in yellow, blue, and white waterfalls. A fresh scent from the herb boxes messages a "thank you" for my recent watering. Often, early in the spring, I carefully prune a window in the grove of trees below so I can view the pond's ducks, geese, and an occasional swan drifting by.

My rooster weathervane is proudly perched in a flourishing Mandevilla. Over this my paradise, sunset colored Hibiscus trees stand as alert sentinels, observing all these lovely color accents. I look over to the Passion Flower, my favorite. Ah! There it is, sitting on a shelf, hanging from the house's yellow siding. Healthy growth blurs its boundaries so it appears to be floating in mid air. Its colors are less striking than its cousins but its persona and shape outshine the others. It is here that I try to capture and store the spiritual energy to sustain me over the rest of the year.

Though not the ardent and expert gardener that my mother was, I experiment each year with different combinations, with some successes. Sometimes I regret a choice or two for having done the disagreeable— dying or looking like a starving child. It is then I fend off regrets, by snipping away at those offending dead plant limbs that have died.

The Passion Flower thrills me beyond comprehension. Its intricate beauty as astounding as the makings of a fine watch, with each part doing its job. It is to me an absolute wonder which inspires instant emotion of love. Why I do identify with this mystifying plant? Maybe, it throws me back to times I am awestruck. I remember times when I was struck by a parent's face resting, perhaps contemplating their life, an animal poised in the stillness of nature, a painting that calls you in. Crystal moments of emotion sear into the mind and heart.

Beyond the face of this exotic flower, the story is in its naming. A group of Roman Catholic priests were on pilgrimage in South America, when they discovered the plant growing on the road. Upon inspection, they named it

Passiflora Incarnate. A rough translation is "flower embodying the Passion of Christ or suffering and death of Christ." A lower set of petals represent the ten Apostles, except Peter, the Denier, and Judas, the Betrayer. The hair-like rays, often purple, remind us of the purple robe and thorny crown that Jesus was forced to wear as the King of the Jews. The stamens and the anthers qualify as the nails from the cross, with the two vine tendrils representing the whips that the mass used on Christ on his way to his execution.

As this year my usual supplier did not order the Passion Flower vines in time, I am afraid that I would not be graced with its beauty. Persistence allowed me to save one of my plants. Not only beautiful, it is used to alleviate depression, insomnia, and other medical woes. Just looking at it, I feel my troubles melting away. While not particularly religious, I still take a look around me and give thanks for those sacrifices by me and others that have brought me this peaceable kingdom and the passion to adore it. Passion is more than romantic notion. Its true meaning is suffering. It is the willingness to suffer for a cause and become victorious. Isn't this the meaning of "living?"

Part 6

ROOMS

BACK AGAIN
Stephen Capizzano

Close your eyes
open your mind
to the memories of a place
where you would always go.

The door that let you in,
how it opened.

The pieces of furniture,
their condition
feel.
Lit by a window, perhaps many.

A picture on the wall that brings you
back to a distant time

The sounds in the room
The colors
smells.

Sit in a chair,
feel the sensation of that touch,
the pressure
the warmth
between your bottom and that chair.

You are back in that room
Because your body still remembers
You never left.

ROOMS OF MY OWN
Jane Barstow

I'm not the typical OCD patient. I don't hoard, I'm not fanatic about cleanliness, the piles of paper on my desk rarely get placed in files. What I do obsess about is the arrangement of my living room furniture. I am compulsive about where each piece goes in repeated attempts to find the best, the most attractive, most appropriate, and most efficient use of space. Genetics and hormones are probably to blame. My mother may have kept the same furniture in exactly the same spot for 50 years but she also emptied ashtrays before anyone was finished smoking and made sure each and every window had its shade pulled to the exact same height. And my daughters, themselves, compulsive rearrangers, understood at an early age the connection between my sudden interior decorating urges and my monthly cycle. The mania has subsided some with age but not entirely.

Most every piece of furniture in my house is regularly on the move and also has its own back story. Before I attempt to bring them to life, I shall set the stage by describing the three interconnected rooms in which they have at various times resided. These are big rooms with canvas ceilings, solid wood pocket doors, and crown molding. The dining room has the most formal woodwork and has seen the fewest major reorganizations. The front room, that must have served as a parlor for entertaining guests in its youth, has seen the most. Though it was home to a baby grand when we acquired the house forty years ago, it was soon transformed into a playroom for our two-year-old daughter. Connecting these two rooms is our main living room with a fireplace and a south facing bay that we filled with plants in true 1970s fashion. These are all long gone allowing us to enjoy the sunlight ourselves.

A few pieces have at various times lived in each of the three rooms. The solid oak cabinet discovered beside the road in Mystic, its claw feet and lions' heads obscured by layers of red paint, first served as a buffet in the dining room. Displaced by my mother's dining room set, which moved in with her, it was transformed into a stereo credenza. Each new placement meant finding a new spot for speakers as well and rerouting wires through the basement and back up to the living room, not a simple task. The upright piano, with its beautiful carvings and warped sounding board lovingly and aggressively restored by a trio of musicians, swapped places with the buffet on several occasions. It required the entire family to lift it onto a rug and slide it across the wood floor. The fainting couch, shabby and so very inviting for afternoon naps, fit into living room spaces vacated by piano or buffet until it collapsed under the weight of a former, too fat friend.

There are two additional pieces about which I am particularly obsessive. First is the Victorian sofa we long coveted and finally inherited from prickly Uncle Norman when his third wife demanded he get rid of it. Uncle Norman bought the sofa while living in England and shipped it back to Connecticut with a crate full of furniture. Elegant and uncomfortable, it is upholstered in a velvety rich green and framed in carved mahogany. We have tried using it as a normal sofa, but guests had to be instructed on how to sit so that they were leaning toward each other. Few managed to strike the right pose without looking awkward. After being placed in at least four different locations, our special sofa now sits in the front corner of what was once the parlor, where it can be seen but not used.

The second piece that has driven me to distraction in recent years plays a far more active role in our living room. A rustic cocktail table made out of a solid slab of walnut, it too has traveled across the Atlantic but via air freight after being driven by friends from Bulgaria to England. Walnut trees are a protected species in Bulgaria. It requires official permission to cut one down and the trunks must be milled. And so we were given the huge slab by a neighbor, which our carpenter offered to make into a bench. How could we leave it behind when we sold our Bulgarian house? Thanks to friends, we didn't have to. But when we finally were able to bring it home from Bradley Airport, it quickly became clear that it didn't seem to belong. It lasted less than a week before Oriental rugs had to be swapped and a new sofa purchased. Now it happily holds drinks and hors d'oeuvres when we have company, books and newspapers when we're on our own. There have been very few additional evenings spent moving other pieces of furniture around since it arrived—it has stayed put. Might it be that I have finally achieved satisfaction and can put my interior decorating compulsion to rest? I doubt it. There's always my daughter's house to rearrange when I visit her.

Part 7

ABUSE AND INJUSTICE

WHAT ARE YOUR INTENTIONS
Wendy Bradford

I, the companion, who rides
the coat-tails of your success.
Yet when reversal of fortune cloaks you,
I slip away from your side and say
"your misfortune nullifies my friendship."

I am the one and truest Believer,
denying another's faith
fitting beyond my divine altar.
I will burn you crying "Heretic
off to the Valley of Death, you go."

I, the leader, dominate the weak
and disabled with false promises.
Trampling upon others
ascends me higher to
the throne of Power.

I am the woman whose machinations
come in an avalanche of helplessness
Like the scorpion, I sting my rescuers
rendering them impotent as I have
sucked the marrow from their bones.

I, the child bully, torments surrounding youth
crushing their dreams in the playground dirt.
This I do to hide the terror I have learned
from adults who have also drunk
from the well of fear.

I am the actor whose facade
Masks my real purpose.

My every action carefully planned will still
betray my real desires.
for, I am Hypocrite.

To Hypocrite, I now respond to your
many confessions, faces, and names.
If only foretelling had been my gift,
I would have stepped off your path,
unscathed by the False Friend,
the Dishonest Apostle,
the Would Be King,
the Damsel in Distress,
and the Vexing Brat.

So what are your intentions
Will you find more martyrs to persecute
or
will you pass them in your travels unscathed?

I know for myself
I am forewarned
My intentions are to travel only
with the trustworthy.

SAINT TERESA AND JESUS
Katherine Marotta

Saint Teresa holds red roses
Jesus hangs crucified on the white brick wall
Together they bless the altar in the tiny Brazilian chapel
Two white wooden benches face them, waiting for Prayers
A Prayer would like it here
Round leaded glass windows slightly opened direct the light of day the only
color offered
I sit and remember when Saint Teresa hung above my bed
Each night I was told she blessed me if I offered her my childhood kisses
Today I sit
I am a Prayer
No kisses, just tears that run trying to forgive
My brother kissed Jesus crucified every night above his bed
perhaps a Prayer assuming forgiveness

THOU ART THE MAN
Peggy Conti

Narcissus.
it is your vastness
expanding arms bow-like
filling door jams
end-to-end

I follow you through woodland
and galleria calling your name...

your name

gaze a preening at each body of water
multiplying your reflection
in every shard of glass

attend hard luck
words that blow from
thin lips of double dealing

through a slender piece of light
watch as you dance
honey mouthed in blackness
with your courtesan

smoothing tongue over
perfectly aligned teeth

poise with pleas
of consent,
I collect only
raw bones

as you grow hollow and diminish
I vault to a dance of danger
with the God of Vengeance
whistling black magic in
your vacant ear

Narcissus, Narcissus
you are the man
you are the man

thou art the dusty old man

TIL DEATH DO US PART

Jane Barstow

I so want to leave but I can't. At first it seemed his self-absorption had simply gotten worse with age. He had always been narcissistic, admiring his own legs rather than mine when we danced. Now when guests arrived, he insisted they come see his latest collage before he took their coats or offered drinks. His office was filled with photos of himself, none of the kids or grandkids. And he no longer made polite conversation, instead telling the same three jokes again and again. Every time he saw a woman with relatively light colored hair, he launched into his blond joke, at the supermarket, on the playground, at a concert. *It's like he has Tourette's*, said my daughter. We all laughed. I told a friend if we were ten years younger, I'd be gone.

Then the symptoms became more obvious: the long time friends he no longer recognized, the confusion about family relationships, the loss of what had been a strong sense of direction. The diagnosis of dementia helped some but not enough. His self-absorption got worse, his dependency on me more and more annoying. He wanted me with him every minute of the day. *What should I eat, has the mail come yet, where can we go*, he asked again and again. The social worker explained I must structure his day, keep him busy, tell him not ask him what to do. So I found him volunteer work at Food Share, I got him simple jigsaw puzzles, I gave him household chores. Still, every day in between reporting on his bowel movements, he would demand I find activity for him. And most every day after the third or fourth time he whined about being bored, I'd lose my temper, "I cannot be responsible for every minute of your day." I so don't want to be a caretaker.

After the diagnosis, I called an acquaintance whose husband had recently died after long suffering from Alzheimer's. She had lots of advice. Take photos of all your friends, lay out four sets of clothes, have him carry a GPS tracker. *How did you manage to stay sane*, I asked. *Well it helped*, she replied, *that my daughter moved home*. Not an option in my case. And how long from diagnosis to his passing? *Seven long years*, was her answer. I so want to leave but I can't.

THE DATE
Anonymous

You love movies. Me too, especially on the big screen under the night sky. My childhood memories of watching movies from the hood of our giant boat-like Plymouth are priceless. "There's a drive-in here in the Fort." My excitement comes through the phone as I say yes to a plan to see the latest adventure packed film on Saturday night.

You pick up a portable dinner. You thoughtfully choose a place offering wraps and fresh veggies.

As you pull in close to the car speaker, I am watching a couple in the Jeep behind us reverse pull in to a speaker then create an actual *outdoor living room*: first a small sofa, then a coffee table, and finally snacks. Then a noisy family of six pull in beside us as the movie starts. Little kids periodically launch themselves in and out of the rear and side windows like an acrobatic troupe.

Midway through the movie you suggest getting a snack; I didn't realize how important a box of popcorn could become....

Small talk, getting to know one another better, talking about careers, family, interests. You ask, "Want some of this?" I turn in my seat; your jeans are down around your knees.

I am frozen. My mind begins to churn slowly through an escape. The road isn't walkable in the dark; it's far from a main road; with no moon, it's dark and scary with coyotes and other unimaginable creatures roaming the Colorado foothills. Friends are out of town and the snack bar closed. I feel trapped and scared.

Had I said something to bring this on? The popcorn box and I became one as I hugged the passenger door. My focus on the ending of the movie can only be described as infrared. The movie ends, and I still can't recall the outcome of the epic battle.

You start the car, uttering something about not seeing the second feature, and drive slowly following other cars out to the road. I am terrified.

At the restaurant parking lot where I'd left my car, I try to remain calm. My dad's motto runs through my brain: *never let 'em see you sweat*. I'm not sure this was the kind of situation he was referencing but I couldn't get out of the car fast enough. My hands shake as I fumble with my car keys, dropping them on the ground. I hear you roll down your window and yell, "I'll call you tomorrow."

"I don't think that's a good idea," I say as I jump in the car and lock all doors.

Years later, as I considered online dating again after breaking off a long-term relationship, yes, someone contacted me. It's you—same photo, same tag line and probably same game. Delete...delete...delete!

BLUE COLLAR WOMEN BLUES
Peggy Conti

here you are
open mouth
arch tongue
swollen

the bossman

a viper savoring my flesh
with a blistering fusion of words
snapping my bones at every consonant

sitting at my workbench soldering
mirrored boxes I buff compound
into shiny gemstones

through this chemical haze
that wraps in poison, I offer
patrician ladies juju beads

to dangle from swan-like necks
as they glitter fire in red brick manors
while I am forced to live a penny a gross

soon night will descend
with a devil's writ...
and borne of inequities

a proclamation...

tomorrow at high noon
a rendering by Caravaggio
with demands for a better hell

and now... allow the bloodletting to begin

PREDATORY MEN AND ME
Jane Barstow

Today it would certainly be called sexual harassment. At the time I thought Lee's behavior simply annoying and slightly embarrassing, sort of like adolescent acne that was hard to treat but eventually went away. We were both often at the office late Friday afternoons, me working on my thesis, Lee dealing with department paperwork. Every time we met in the hall, he would touch me on the shoulder, on my arm, running his hand down my back. I asked a younger colleague what it meant. *Not to worry*, he assured me, *it's like football players tapping each other's buttocks as they leave the field*. Perhaps not quite the right analogy.

But I'm getting ahead of my history here. My experience with predatory men actually started at the age of five when my great Uncle Sam would sit me on his knee and run his tongue around my ear. Weird. Everyone thought Uncle Sam was weird anyway. Then there was the flasher in the park and the rain-coated men in the movie theater. By the age of eight, my friends and I knew to move away when we saw one come near us. By the age of thirteen, I had experienced wild packs of teenage boys who enjoyed terrorizing every girl who crossed their paths.

As a young woman teaching in Japan, I usually felt perfectly safe until one night a man jumped into my taxicab and started pawing at me. The driver ignored my protests so I jumped out at the first traffic light. Moving on to Paris, things got worse and worse: goosing in the metro, catcalls in the street, and ultimately a real scare as a fellow foreign student climbed through my bedroom window. Fortunately for me but not for him, he quickly climbed back out falling five stories through an open courtyard. Apparently he was deterred by the curlers in my hair and not my screams which no one claimed to have heard.

Back in the USA and sleeping soundly in my own bed, I was delighted to get a job as a translator and editor for the Encyclopedia Britannica in Chicago. I loved the work, appreciated the praise and encouragement I got from my boss until one day while we were both watching the astronauts parade down Michigan Avenue, I felt his hand on my thigh. *Please stop*, I insisted as firmly as I could, but stop he did not. I walked out the door and never came back again. This was in July of 1969; I had just turned 24. Three years later I was married, starting an academic career and along came Lee. *What is it about me*, I began to wonder. Is it because I'm so small or is it some vibe I somehow emit? I had been a bit of a party girl, but nothing too wild.

Oh, Lee. I have so many stories about you. The time you invited my husband and me to your ski chalet and ruined a lovely day by joking that you were going to make love to me for hours on end. If only I had been quick witted enough to retort, "you wouldn't last for more than twenty minutes." The time we were both standing in the department office and you suddenly grabbed me by the breasts and swung me around the office. The time you invited me for a drink to discuss our "issues," then asked if I was attracted to the boys in my classes. "I'm happily married," I stupidly replied. If only I had been quick witted enough to retort, "not the boys." It was my male colleagues who suggested the retorts when I shared these stories. They also encouraged me to "lean in," to stand in front of the room when making a report, and to be sure to wear my highest heels. None of this stopped Lee from walking directly in front of me when I got up to speak. Let me be clear here. Lee supported my career, he never used my demurrals or embarrassment against me. I was annoyed but not damaged by his behavior. His wife divorced him for far worse transgressions. So where is the line between teasing and genuine harassment? No question that Lee abused a position of power, that he was a masher and a womanizer. But he was not violent, he was not a rapist.

By the age of thirty-five, my encounters with predatory men seemed over with little lasting impact. My aversion to anyone playing with my ears did continue. For a while after the Paris attack, I had trouble sleeping alone and suffered from occasional nightmares, but these subsided after a few years. I once asked a class of twenty-five young women how many had ever had an unpleasant encounter with a stranger; almost every hand went up and we all laughed and cried at the stories we shared. The Boston Globe columnist Ellen Goodman wryly noted that women must pay a premium to live in neighborhoods where they feel safe walking at night. My own daughter was mugged in Brooklyn, by teenage girls as it happens. Is there a conclusion to be drawn here? The Me Too movement has led many of us to revisit our own more or less traumatic histories with predatory males. But let's be careful to distinguish between the true bad guys: the aggressive harassers, the rapists, the pedophiles, the murderers as opposed to the simple jerks—between the men we should laugh at and the ones we should lock up. And let's do all we can to raise boys who respect women rather than prey on them.

BOUNDARIES
Anonymous

Happy families, siblings gathering for summer picnics
Laughing, crying, celebrating life's moments together
Where did it end?
Homeless at sixty
Bad decisions followed by more bad decisions
Is there a way out of this rabbit hole?
What are the boundaries for sibling love?
Until you can no longer breathe?
Or until you join him in the hole?
Anger wages war inside me
Stop.
Tough love, a fleeting thought
As I write to tell him I've given enough
Can give no more
The cycle of caring never stops
From one disaster to another
I see the happy gatherings
And wonder, is there more?

Part 8

QUESTS

THE GIVEAWAY
Emma Weiss

Everyone wants to earn their way in
a trip down the slot
of the giveaway box
to point elsewhere
or Regals sound.
That dollar may even help you hedge your bets
against the incoming tide.
And in the days and hours to come
and within all the little minutes that make them up
everyone's green will gather.
Unpocketed then unfurled
these little sails of commerce
floating in an empty sea of small barcodes
the entry slips a waiting flotilla
in a Kraft paper box
piling up along with the hopes
of a win
in a Red Chevy sweepstakes.
Entrants dreaming of
borders to cross and
lines to invent onto the road
in melting August rubber.
Then gliding under a glowering sun that splits open blacktop
like the eye of Horus
splits open the road in Texas or Reno somewhere.
Hot Egyptian eye on the hood
of a deep summer hour
that goes glinting off pinstripes and chrome
melting the fleeting roads
beneath the endless American dream.

ANCIENT QUESTS
Al Clemence

Migration has been a part of the history of mankind, since men first walked out of Africa in search of the resources to sustain their families.

When the world was an empty place, these migratory quests were honored as explorations. Those who led the way were praised as heroes. Even today we honor their memories and speak of them with reverence.

When we imagine the nearby planets and dream of the places yet to be discovered, do we still think of those who will lead the way as heroes or are they now thought of as migrants who will spread evil and disease throughout the universe?

Will the revered explorers, who find pathways to the future, become reviled for spreading disease with each footstep? When did exploration become migration and migration become immigration?

The population of the earth is now approaching eight billion. It is unclear how many of us can be sustained by the remaining resources. Are we destined to return to a system of feudalism where large bands of armed men and women compete violently for what resources remain?

A brief trip aboard the International Space Station would inform us that the areas of the earth that can sustain us comfortably are already filled with people. Migration no longer occurs into empty lands. Migration has become immigration. The search for and control of remaining resources is no longer a friendly competition.

If we should, by chance, find ourselves in the shoes of those who humbly stand before "beautiful" walls—walls built by those who feared the loss of something that was beyond their understanding—could we convince those on the other side that they need not fear us? Could we convince them that we also were victims of an ancient strategy, that had been instinctively practiced, but which was no longer valid?

How could we convince those who block our path that their wall is also an ancient strategy that is no longer valid. The political screed that passes for reason is flawed. What moral matrix will be postulated to justify actions that reason cannot defend?

JOURNEY FROM BELCHATOW
Andy Rosenzweig

Where do we come from? Is it important to know? The curiosity with this journey called life, and delving into our roots, is lately becoming an obsession with some.

> ...thousands of ants creeping on top of the Empire State Building. The ants probably were carried there by winds or birds, but nobody is sure; nobody in New York knows any more about the ants than they do about the panhandler who takes taxis to the Bowery; or the dapper man who picks trash out of Sixth Avenue trash cans. (Gay Talese, "New York Is a City of Things Unnoticed")

Not exactly the immigrant experience, especially in the age of Ancestry.com and DNA. Early this year, in 2019, I found out I had relatives who died in the Holocaust. The knowledge of this immediately gripped me. It began as a result of my daughter Jane's interest in knowing more about where she came from. Ergo a DNA test through Ancestry. The test provoked a response from the company asking if she wanted to be put in touch with a woman in Sweden with whom she shared a significant amount of alleles in their DNA.

Not too much later Ann Olsson and I began an email relationship. My cousin (second or third?) was on her own journey to find out more about her mother's history. Her mother had the number 44889 tattooed on her left forearm. She had always been reluctant ("too sad") to talk much about her history. She did reveal to Ann that she'd been liberated from Ravensbrück in 1945, but her own parents perished earlier while they were all imprisoned at Auschwitz.

Turns out that Ann's quite a competent investigator. So much so that she and her husband traveled to Belchatow, Poland this past spring to see what she could uncover about our shared history. That's the small town in Poland (part of Russia in the early 20th century) where her mother and my father were born.

In one of our email exchanges, I told Ann about a story my father told me late in his life (he died in 2000 at the age of ninety-three.) It was a curiosity to me. The reason being that I'd spent a good part of my life and career tracking down killers and other bad men and bringing them to justice. Turns out, my father's grandparents according to family lore, were murdered by "highwaymen" in the old country. The eight or nine Rosenzweig children—or Rosenczwaig in Ann's history—were scattered about Eastern Europe after that.

My father's journey from Belchatow to America took place in 1909 when he was three-years-old. He recalled coming over "in steerage" on a ship called the Arabaic, with his older brother Sam and his mother Eva (her name was actually Chanie or Chawa according to Ann's investigation). Abe Rosenzweig had arrived several years earlier and again, according to my father's memory, he had to be pressured to bring over his wife and children. It didn't end happily. Not too many years later, when my father wasn't yet a teenager, Abe abandoned the family for greener pastures—for Texas of all places. He returned to New York in the 1930s and died of cancer not much later.

Irving left school in the seventh or eighth grade to go to work on the Lower East Side of Manhattan, for a fruit and vegetable peddler. His pay was a bag of produce, which must have been treasure to a near starving family of four. (Aunt Shirley was born a few years after the Ellis Island arrival in 1909.)

The Soviets liberated Ravensbrück on April 29 and 30, 1945. Approximately 3,500 extremely ill prisoners lived at the camp. The Nazis had sent the other remaining women on a death march. It is estimated that 50,000 women died at Ravensbrück, either from harsh living conditions, slave labor, or they were executed.

Ann Olsson's mother and so many other survivors of the atrocities must have fought hard to survive. The following passage found through an Internet search may explain how she eventually found herself in Sweden.

Count Folke Bernadotte, vice president of the Swedish Red Cross, had convinced Heinrich Himmler to allow the International Red Cross to rescue some prisoners from Ravensbrück and other camps and bring them to Sweden. The Swedish Red Cross was first allowed to rescue Scandinavians on March 5, followed by women from France, Poland, and the Benelux countries.

Through the intervention of the Swedish section of the World Jewish Congress, Bernadotte requested that Jewish prisoners also be sent to Sweden. Himmler agreed, and between April 22 and April 28, about 7,500 women — an estimated 1,000 of them Jewish — were liberated from Ravensbrück. They were then ferried from Copenhagen to Malmö in neutral Sweden. Once there, they received clothing, food, and medical attention and were then sent to recuperate in different locations. Afterward, most of the non-Jewish women returned to their homelands. The Jewish women sought out surviving family members in their former homelands, but most immigrated to Israel or the Americas, and some settled in Sweden.

It's the images of the women that most affected me today at the Museum of Jewish Heritage. They were garbed in little more than rags and the enlarged black and white photographs on poster boards showed faces of abject sadness. Many of them held their children in their arms, some by the hands. And in some of the printed words accompanying the displays are descriptions of the children being forcibly taken from their mothers for a fate few could have imagined.

Sound familiar? The separation of small children from their parents for no real reason other than they were "others."

Today, July 22, 2019 my daughters Jane and Lynn and I visited the museum in lower Manhattan, in Battery Park. Visible from the western side of the property are Liberty and Ellis Islands. It had been 22 years since I last visited the stark looking light brown stone and glass building. That was before the Museum opened, which happened some weeks later.

The man who spearheaded the creation of the Museum was Robert M. Morgenthau. By then he'd been the District Attorney of Manhattan for twenty-two years and for twelve of those years, I'd been his Chief Investigator. He had asked me one day to visit and report back on the quality of the security system. That was the last time I'd visited the museum until this past Monday. Coincidentally (or perhaps oddly) Bob Morgenthau died the day before our visit, just days shy of his hundredth birthday.

And now, Monday July 22, 2019 I wander through the Auschwitz exhibit with my daughters. It would be meaningful and weighty enough that I'm a Jew with a rich immigrant history, and one who only recently learned that I (we) have relatives who lived through or perished in the Holocaust. That would be enough to dwell on, to occupy the meaning of life.

But now I'm left to wonder what it might mean that the man who was not only my long-time boss and a father figure to me, died the day before our visit (which had been planned a month earlier). What am I to make of all this?

There was a bit of back and forth in the days leading up to our visit, about where my girls would take me to lunch for my seventy-fifth birthday, which is only days away. Lynn, very adept on her iphone (if that's what it is?) made and cancelled a couple of reservations at nearby restaurants. We discovered on the way out of the museum, the lovely little Lox Café that features traditional Jewish fare: a variety of lox dishes, potato latkes, borscht, chocolate babka or black and white cookies for dessert, and so forth. Reminded us of the long gone Ratner's dairy restaurants on Delaney Street (or the one on Second Avenue) on the Lower East Side of Manhattan. A destination where so many Eastern European Jews ended up in the early twentieth century, through fate, or luck, or grit, or through some other divine intervention?

We missed out on one thing during the Museum visit: their sound system was down and we didn't have the benefit of the narration of the experience by survivors of the Holocaust. Though personally, I didn't need to hear the words. As I looked at elderly men and women from a variety of countries who survived the latest diaspora of Jews—this wasn't the first in the thousands of years of our shared experience—I could easily understand and "listen to" the pathos as they described surviving the worst of mankind's behavior.

We're blessed to be here, every day, and none of us should ever forget that. As the Torah says, "choose life."

Jane photographed a passage written by Charlotte Delbo an Auschwitz survivor, that hangs on the wall of the Museum. It seems the right coda to this story:

> You who are passing by
> I beg you
> Do something
> Learn a dance step
> Something to justify your existence
> Something that gives you the right
> To be dressed in your skin in your body hair
> Learn to walk and to laugh
> Because it would be too senseless
> After all
> For so many to have died
> While you live
> Doing nothing with your life

— Auschwitz survivor Charlotte Delbo (1971)

Part 9

PREJUDICE

AN UNIMAGINED SLICE OF MEXICO
Phoebe Huang

Some of my favorite trips have included stays at the Hotel Monasterio in Cusco, Peru, alongside the Inkaterra Machu Picchu; the Lizard Island Resort in Australia, Caneel Bay, before the hurricane; the Schweitzerhof in Bern Switzerland; and the Ahwahnee Hotel, Yosemite National Park. Each is unique in its architecture, setting, ambiance, hospitality.

Now, I have to add the Presidente Intercontinental, on Cozumel.

I had doubts about going to Mexico. The stories of hijackings, tourist muggings were more than deterring. However, a mother/daughter trip to visit the Mayan ruins, snorkeling in the Marine Preserve, and escaping winter were just too appealing. Contrary to expectation, we experienced the most gracious hospitality, a slice of Mexico not previously imagined.

That Cozumel is an island reachable only by water keeps it out of the fray that surrounds Cancun, and other coastal towns. We also arranged for car service from the airport to the Cozumel ferry, thereby eliminating any risk posed by anonymous taxis. The key decision, however, was choosing the Presidente Intercontinental.

As our car pulled up to the boom barrier blocking entry to the resort, and a young man walked out of the guardhouse with a clipboard, I turned to my daughter, "...the moment of truth." I have been known to botch reservations. There was the time I waited for my daughter's flight at Kona International Airport. The flight deplaned, but no Wendy. I had, without thinking, made the reservation in her maiden name. Much explanation and many hours later, she was allowed to board a flight to the Big Island.

On still another occasion, I made two reservations on Cathay Airlines in my name, had to cancel one with penalty, and rebook the second reservation properly.

So, when the young man came out, asked for our name, and affirmed that we were actually on his list of reservations, we were "home free."

The pleasure of this trip only increased from there.

The security around the Presidente freed us entirely from thinking about our personal safety or about losing something of value — particularly our laptops.

My daughter learned through anecdote how seriously this security is taken. A group of invitees to a wedding held at the resort stayed at other hotels on the island. The hosts assumed they could invite all these people, post wedding, to come and enjoy the Presidente facilities/amenities. However, the hotel permitted only a few family members; they could not vouch for unregistered guests, and could not compromise the security of those legitimately registered. This sounded like a prudent policy to me.

Among many wonderful memories from this trip, two will remain with me. First was the service. We're not talking about waiters hovering four feet from the table. No, this was the graceful effort everywhere to show us a face of Mexico at odds with the stereotype. If this was a result of excellent hospitality training, I applaud it. But my take away is that these were people aching to be proud of their country, and wanting visitors to know who they really are.

My impression was reinforced. A young boy, maybe nine or ten, was planting his football ball into a hollow of sand, and kicking it to an older boy he seemed to know. My son is an athlete; so I watched this ball play with interest. When he sat down on the chaise near me, I complimented him on his ball skills and we got into conversation.

"Did you see the entertainment last night?" he asked.

"No," I replied, "I'm allergic to bug bites, so I duck in after dark."

"Well, as long as we do the hoo ha's, [he mimicked native dancing, with wild gesticulations of the arms], we'll never be a first-rate country."

Talk about unexpected! He then went on to describe a multi-furcated school system that must exist in countries all over the world — the result of global business. In Mexico City, he explained, there are American, German, French, British, and Japanese schools in addition to the local schools. He attends a German school. His father is Mexican but his mother has German ancestry. Classes are conducted in German, Spanish, and English.

Then, in a total non sequitur, he asked me quite seriously, "Why does Trump hate us so much?"

I had to be honest, "Because he's ignorant. Now you can fix ignorant, but he's not inclined to."

This boy's next comment was the real heartbreaker, "I just wish everyone knew we are not all trying to scramble over the fence to get into your country."

He would possess the intelligence to understand that one person attempting to tar an entire country with the same brush doesn't change who he is — a bright, articulate, forward-thinking young person — or what he stands for. But what of others less fortunate?

It's an old saw that travel broadens the mind. Meeting this young boy and his countrymen/women was certainly broadening for me. Though embarking on this trip, spending time with my daughter was more the focus than opening our eyes to an unforgettable slice of Mexico.

Years ago, a friend mentioned, in passing, that he always made separate and special time for each of his daughters. That casual comment turned me around. Certainly, family trips are meaningful and spending undivided time with each child should have been as obvious. Yet, until Gino's observation, this idea had never occurred to me. I did, though, take it to heart. So, my son and I traveled to Lizard Island and Heron Island to experience the Great Barrier Reef, a destination he had talked about since grade school. Fortunately, we saw four-inch wide Giant Clams with their winking, gem-like eyes, and dozens of coral species before the bleaching devastation. My daughter and I finished the grueling day-long hike to Machu Picchu, along ancient Incan trails, with triumphant smiles and a rainbow; we went to Cozumel, and it goes on.

DISAPPOINTMENT
Mel Jolly

The real question is not 'what were some of your major disappointments in life,' but rather, how did you recognize, react, and recover your ability to move forward. I have seen any number of situations in which unhealthy circumstances took hold of a person, resulting in self-destruction and leading to the inability to work beyond the conditions, thereby affecting the ability to function in what society would consider "normal" behavior.

We know "normal" is a relative term, but it is a starting point – a reference to how well we fit into our structured world. I can recall three major events in my life that resulted in my being disappointed. First, the death of my mother when I was about four-years old....I refuse to research the exact date of her death, because I prefer the haze and fog that surrounds the event. Being such a young child, I didn't understand the loss of my mother, so my sense of disappointment was somewhat delayed. It wasn't until I began to see my friends interact with their mothers that I began to miss the bonding of child and mom. I missed her telling me about girls and how to be respectful, mannerly, and kind. I missed the Mother-to-Son talks.

My second life affecting disappointment began early in my youth but actually lasted for a couple decades. I was ashamed that I was a black child – probably not so much ashamed, but rather disappointed to not always feel accepted. Watching the opportunities made available to some of the kids by virtue of their being white was brutal enough to a child, but even more devastating were the subdivisions among the black population: Skin light or dark, hair straight or kinky, nose and lips broad or thin. My disappointment was the feeling that I was stuck with what I had, even if my particular physical characteristics were not "acceptable" to everyone.

My third major life influencing disappointment was not so much with my viewpoint, but with the vision of society. When I was in high school, at least in my hometown area, the societal concept was that blacks were unintelligent, couldn't learn, and didn't need to learn. A schedule change caused me to be transferred into a new history class, which I discovered was comprised predominately of athletes, the majority of whom were black.

The teacher was having the students read out loud from the textbook when I arrived: I was horrified as one after another of the students stumbled over words, until I realized they could barely read at all. When it came to be my turn, I read only a sentence or two before the teacher stopped me, questioned why I had been assigned to his class, and immediately sent me back to my counselor for yet another transfer. It was then that I understood the thought process that there I was – 'a black kid and an athlete, so okay, he must be a slow learner, so put him in the remedial class.'

The disappointment from the scenario came to me that day as I walked down my high school hallway and wondered what would happen to all the others in the class. The expectations were low for those students, but in hindsight, in that class of 'slow learners' was the Indiana State #1 Basketball Player who went on to college, won a NCAA College Basketball Championship, and then was selected #2 Draft Choice by the Boston Celtics. If you could run fast, jump high, or put the ball in the basket, you were 'taken care of' – the college or the professional team could use you.

But on the other hand, so many young people were discarded early in life, never having the chance to find out what they could – or should – do. That to me is the biggest disappointment: Lives unlived or stopped before the game begins.

FREEDOM
Stephen Capizzano

Once upon a time there was an old man who lived on a very small boat. Every evening he would anchor his boat alongside a rather much larger more elegant boat in the harbor. When he did, he would look up to the larger boat waiting to give a greeting to the owner should he appear. Limited in most things, the size of the boat being one of many, the old man was nevertheless carefree. He saw joy everywhere and would devotedly stand on the bow in the evening waiting for the owner of the larger boat to appear so as to greet him. But he never came. The old man began to believe that the owner of the larger boat did not live on it and it saddened him to think that such a beautiful boat was not being used to its fullest.

But one evening, as he stood on the bow waiting to greet the owner once again, the old man caught something strange out of the corner of his eye. He noticed a figure moving, hunched over very low, as if not wanting to be seen. And he understood.

CURLY
Katherine Marotta

curly
There I said it
My email says it too
I embrace the gray curls
Once much darker with more of them
The label…"brillo head" is a thing of the past
As is any sense of being ugly
I embrace my curls

SPRING: THE ATHLETES' PERSPECTIVE
Mel Jolly

In some parts of America, four seasons of weather are experienced, whereas in other areas of our country, that is not the case. Having grown up in Indiana, I had the opportunity to see all the changes that identify each season as it arrives. In the athletic world, the changing of the seasons represents the beginning, or the ending of a particular sport. For me, spring denotes, as in nature, a do-over. It is the time when all past successes and failures are brushed aside with the hope of emerging a better performer than the prior year. Therein lies the dream of all competitive athletes: to make the necessary jump to the next highest level of achievement.

In nature, as in the animal kingdom, only the strongest survive, which also is true in the world of athletes. The belief is that only the best will make the cut, but sometimes something strange occurs that seemingly goes against the laws of nature and thus can only be described as a freak of nature. This is particularly true for athletes whose physical appearance defies their performance level.

For my uncle, spring was his favorite time of the year. He loved being outdoors, and in his era, track and field sports only took place outside. My uncle was a tremendous high jumper; he set the Indiana High School record in 1936 by clearing the bar at six feet, six inches. He was a friend of Jesse Owens and Ralph Metcalf, as well as other Olympians, even though he himself did not qualify for the Olympic Team that went to Germany. Fast forward to 1960, and a young man—I will call him Mutt—was competing in the high jump, an event that just happened to be officiated by my uncle. Mutt was a perfect example of an athlete whose ability was a contradiction to his physical appearance. He was only five feet, six inches tall, but he cleared the six feet, six inches bar, thereby matching the record set by my uncle twenty-four years prior. Mutt decided to continue jumping, so the bar was raised to six feet, eight inches. After missing his first two efforts, on his third and final attempt, he cleared the bar and became the state record holder in the high jump, having broken my uncle's long standing record. Mutt had accomplished a feat that completely defied his physical stature. Maybe he was energized because that particular day was full of sunshine and warm temperatures, rather than rain and cold winds that are often associated with early spring.

To athletes, spring means getting outside, being able to run and jump, swing a tennis racket, bat a baseball, or read the greens for putting. For almost everyone, spring means being able to discard heavy coats and gloves in favor of lighter-weight attire. But for the purest, spring means the hand of nature is touching everything around us, giving it new life. It means new smells and colors abound, creating an awakening of the spirit for a brighter tomorrow than it was yesterday. Spring has its effect on all of God's creatures; just as for butterflies, we all change in significant ways, in hopes of being better than we were before. After all, isn't that why we have do-overs every spring?

Part 10

LOVE

TEN YEARS AGO, TODAY
Stephen Capizzano

It was ten years ago today when you spoke that word…and broke my heart. Not an easy thing to do to this confirmed bachelor but I knew the moment it was said, that my life had changed—I just didn't know how much. We met by coincidence, nothing special I thought, but in the eyes of the friend you were with, she saw something.

"That man had a twinkle in his eye for you," she said. Not only did I not see that twinkle but I didn't see you for another year.

But destiny was playing its usual tricks on us when you walked back into my life.

"Lunch?" I said?

"Yes," you said.

What a wonderful word, but no broken heart just yet. That would be for another day.

That I thought we were meant to be together was born strangely out of our separate histories, which unknowingly intertwined: I lived alone on a secluded dirt road in the middle of the woods for twenty years. You, for those twenty years, hiked and snowshoed down that same dirt road and somehow oddly, we never met. *How strange*, you thought when you passed by the cow path that served as my driveway, *who would ever live down there?*

I would!

Destiny continued to play its tricks many years before, when you, as a young girl from another state, began to work in the same town where I grew up, passing the house in which I lived, on your daily trips.

"Dinner?" I said.

"Yes," you said.

And still no broken heart…yet.

We began to see each other more, to see each other more deeply, as we were destined to do, as our histories were compelling us to do. It's just that we didn't know that it was destiny. How could we? We were looking forward, not back where destiny hides. And I, a confirmed bachelor for fifty-seven years, was ready.

"I want to marry you, will you marry me?" I said.

"Yes," you said.

And my heart broke, shattered…with joy, happiness and love. Thank you.

FOR FOREST, FOR TREES

Erik Caswell

I once read in a monologue of Tennessee
Williams' that when a human being
builds a nest in the heart of another
no one thinks whether or not the tree
may someday fall down.
And here I have been with you
bracing myself for the declaration of Timber
practically from day one.
I cannot walk tree to tree when the forest
overwhelms and what kind of hell is it
to be so lost in your own body
not even your touch brings me home
because home is an iron cage
I do not wish to wrest against any longer.
You only wish to help me
but would this still be the case
if I wanted both to lay on your chest
and fly as far as the wind would carry me?
These days I have not been writing
hiding from priorities that will become
my wings. You and I are one more tree
in a forest in which I do not wish to live.
Love is a leap of faith and trust
it is love of something that calls me
                                        to jump.

ICE CREAM:
CHOICE, CRAVING, AND CULTURE
Katharine Leigh

My family celebrated with food. Perhaps the Great Depression had something to do with it. Whatever. The focus here is on my favorite food, you can call it: ICE CREAM. It deserves capital letters because my life would not be complete without it. I LOVE ice cream.

My Mom would steal into the kitchen late on Sunday nights, for a bowl of maple walnut. She would savor each spoonful, then announce she would start her diet in the morning, Monday morning! Maple walnut was never my favorite and I don't recall any of my siblings or Dad ever serving themselves out of her stash—but now as I think back, maybe that's *why* she liked that flavor because a half gallon would be one serving for the six foot, four inch males in the family.

I remember going for a Wednesday afternoon "ride" to look at the ocean, touring through little spots that held clam shacks and yes, ice cream stands. One exploration landed my family at an ice cream stand in Tiverton where I decided to deviate from my usual chocolate selection.

"Ginger," I said as my Dad asked me what flavor I would like.

"Are you sure?" he asked twice.

When my cone was passed to me, I took it to the tables to the side of the stand and sat down to have my first taste. "AAAgggggghhhhhh!" It was awful. Whatever possessed me to try something different?! I dropped my cone in the trash and sat watching my whole family enjoy their selections.

I developed over time my favorite ice cream fix, my treat when I celebrated: coffee ice cream with combinations of peanut butter, chocolate, almonds, caramel…I might deviate and have peach or pistachio, but rarely. There was something about the cold, sweet feel and taste sensation as the flavors awoke on my tongue.

After many years, moving back to the East Coast began the search for ICE CREAM. From May to the beginning of fall, ice cream was plentiful, and I found several locations that met my craving. The little blue house with an order window—they had the best chocolate peanut butter. The convenience store in the north part of town had not only great chocolate peanut butter but coffee soft serve—rare in the West! And if all else failed, there was Dairy Queen's peanut buster parfait. But, when October came, I learned sadly there would be no ice cream stops. Every place closed for winter.

What do good Finnish women crave in the coldest of winter days? ICE CREAM! This was a joke among the men in my family but seriously, there's nothing like ice cream on a cold dreary wintry day! At lunch with Finnish friends, this cultural trait was confirmed as we saved room for dessert—ice cream. My daughters and I carry on this tradition proudly, passing it on to each grandchild and searching out the best ice cream from New Hampshire to Virginia.

Part 11

TRAGEDY

SEPTEMBER DAYS
Al Clemence

A day in early September is often the best time to visit New York City and today we would not be disappointed. My wife, Karen, and I come to the city frequently. We now live in Rhode Island, but the energy and diversity of this city still draw us here several times a year. We were standing on the observation walkway at the top of the Empire State building. The City was spread out below us in sharp detail.

Our first apartment together was located just across the East River in Queens. That was years ago, 1968 in fact. We were both working for the same airline. I was a pilot, who had just been released from military service and Karen had come to New York from St. Louis, Missouri. It was her first assignment as a new flight attendant. For both of us, the city was a magical place, full of promise and expectations.

We were looking across the city toward Battery Park and Staten Island. The Twin Towers of the World Trade Center were gone. As we looked toward the Hudson River, a large airplane appeared above the New Jersey shoreline. We watched as the passenger jet descended to follow the Hudson River toward LaGuardia Airport. In just a few minutes it seemed close enough for us to touch.

It had been several years since that September day when two airplanes had destroyed the Twin Towers. This was the first time since that attack that we had come to this observation deck. We were standing outside on top of what was now the tallest building in the city. Karen squeezed my hand just slightly and I knew that she felt as I did. At this moment, we would rather be somewhere other than this exposed walk way. As we waited for the jet to pass by us, the memory of that September day returned in sharp detail.

A shallow layer of fog had clung to the stanchions of the Throgs Neck Bridge, resting silently just below the suspended roadway. It was 6:30 in the morning and I had nearly completed my daily commute from Connecticut to the Federal Aviation District Office building in Garden City, NY. As I drove out of the fog at the highest section of the bridge, I entered a world populated by only the tallest buildings of the New York landscape. In front of me, a large flock of seagulls, startled by my approach, filled the air, flying gracefully above and below me. For the briefest of moments, I felt that I had joined them in their flight. The only witnesses to my extraordinary feat were the Twin Towers of the World Trade Center that stood guarding passage into the City of New York. On the far side of the bridge, the roadway again descended into the fog, pulling me with it and away from my fantasy of flight.

Twenty minutes later, I was seated at my desk on the fifth floor of a contemporary office building. The window above my desk faced west. It provided an unobstructed view of Manhattan. That day, the visibility in the city was unlimited, the sky was cloudless; it was a perfect September morning in New York.

My world and that of all Americans was about to be shocked as abruptly and painfully as a burn from spattered cooking oil.

At 9:38, a murmur of speculation spread through the office. There was smoke coming from the north side of one of the Twin Towers. The room became quiet. No one was willing to be the first to offer an explanation. After several false starts, a consensus developed that a small airplane had struck the North Tower. It seemed improbable, since the location of the impact was far below the top of the building, which would have required intent or extreme negligence by the pilot.

I tried to return to my normal work schedule, which included preparations for a scheduled pilot evaluation. However, thirty minutes later, when the second airplane struck the South Tower, that became impossible.

As I drove from my office in Garden City, to JFK Airport in Jamaica, Queens, there was already a noticeable change in everything around me. Fire trucks and emergency equipment were racing toward Manhattan. The air was filled with the sounds of sirens and the roar of engines. There was a sense of fear and uncertainty that seemed almost palpable.

I arrived at the operations office for North American Airlines at the JFK Airport without incident. From the parking lot, I could clearly see the Twin Towers, which were less than ten miles away across Jamaica Bay. Both towers displayed large plumes of smoke rising straight up into the sky. The air was calm and the scene around me was uncommonly quiet. People spoke in soft tones. We seemed to be watching a giant silent movie—a movie that had no script and for which no conclusion had been written.

I knew that the scene in those buildings would be one of extreme anxiety as men and women tried to understand what was happening above and below them. The impact from the airplanes had sprayed one hundred thousand pounds of aviation fuel across two floors of the buildings. The explosion that followed incinerated everyone and everything in its path. The resulting fire burned with an intensity that melted steel. The fuel that had not been ignited in the explosion was cascading down stairways and elevator shafts in a futile attempt to escape from the flames that followed it. For those who remained, the race for survival had begun. Shoulder to shoulder they filled the stairways. In determined silence, they stepped away from their fear. The sounds from the heavy tread of helmeted heroes echoed far below. Hope rose along this path to life and passed from one to another until it faced the flames above. There it lingered. Long moments passed. Then, first with a whisper and then with a roar, hope was gone. The Twin Towers were gone. Like a sound replaced by silence, they were simply gone. More than three thousand people perished in just moments.

Now, as Karen and I watch the passenger jet continue up the Hudson River and make a turn for a landing at LaGuardia, Airport, my thoughts return to our plans for today. As we wait for the elevator that will take us to rejoin the intensity of life on the streets below, the memory of that September day remains behind with those who shall always be remembered there.

SIMPLY GONE
Al Clemence

Gone is the security of that distant horizon beyond which we would not see.
Gone the vast oceans that once sheltered you and me
Gone from the sky, two pillars of power now prostrate lie.
On the streets below, the steel and stones that once stood tall are but clouds of dust racing away.
Racing through the alleys, racing down the streets, racing away.
Like sounds replaced by silence.
Simply Gone.

SAY "AAH" LIEUTENANT
Hugh M. Ryan

John Coll and I met in August, 1966, standing in a serpentine line of about 200 newly minted second lieutenants in the United States Army, as we wended our way through the induction physical exam at Aberdeen Proving Grounds, Maryland, home of the Ordnance Corps. We were all dressed (or undressed) identically—it was, after all, the Army—in underwear shorts, black Army dress socks, and black, spit-polished, Army dress shoes. Nothing more. We were entering the Ordnance Officers' Basic Course, our first duty station.

The small gymnasium was spotted with a dozen or so card tables spaced several feet from each other. We progressed from station to station, doctor to doctor, orthopedist, cardiologist, ophthalmologist, etc., assisted by assorted nurses and technicians. I thought we must have made a comical sight—200 male twenty-somethings, traipsing dutifully along in our underwear shorts and street shoes. To me, it evoked that classic nightmare.

A close college friend of mine had alerted me that John would be in my class at this course. He knew of John through a mutual friend, but never having met John himself, could not describe John's appearance to me. I had just his name tucked away in my memory and I knew that John had graduated from Boston College the same day my friend and I graduated from Georgetown, sister Jesuit universities of a sort. Also, like me, he had been commissioned via R.O.T.C.

Chatting with the fellow behind me in line, I noticed that he was wearing a class ring that resembled mine in design, but with a maroon stone. I knew B.C.'s colors were maroon and gold.

"Is that a B.C. ring?" I asked.

"Yes," he replied, slightly surprised. "You didn't go to B.C., did you?"

"No, I went to Georgetown. So, if you went to B.C., you must be John Coll."

At that instant, I learned that "his jaw dropped" is not merely a figure of speech, because John's jaw quite literally dropped. He stood stock still for a couple of seconds, jaws agape, eyes wide, looking like a total fool, as I suppressed my laughter.

Finally, he managed to sputter, "How do you know my name?"

"Oh, I don't know. I'm kind of intuitive that way."

"What?!? No, you aren't."

"Apparently, I am."

I played out the string for a couple of minutes, then confessed to the heads-up I'd been given. To paraphrase Humphrey Bogart's Rick Blaine character, it was the start of a beautiful friendship. We completed the Ordnance Officers' Basic Course by mid-October, then were dispatched together to the Army Supply Officers' Course at Fort Lee, Virginia, from which we graduated in December.

Over those four months, we became close friends. We had been raised by similar families in similar communities, attended the same types of schools, and been inculcated with the same values. Our attitudes about striving, self-reliance, and responsibility, love and death, God, family, and country were not similar; they were identical. We were even both engaged to intelligent, beautiful brunettes with sweet dispositions, still matriculating through Catholic women's colleges, one near B.C. and the other near Georgetown, men's colleges at the time. When I reflect on those days, John and I look to me so much alike that it is almost scary.

After Fort Lee, I was stationed first at a depot across the Susquehanna River from Harrisburg, Pennsylvania, and then, at the height of the Vietnam War, in Korea.

When my commanding officer in Pennsylvania notified me of my deployment, I said, "Korea? That was the last war. You mean I'm going to Vietnam."

"No, lieutenant, I do know the difference. You're going to Korea."

I was stationed at Camp Carroll Depot, about 200 miles south of Seoul. My summary of my military service in Asia is that I fought the Tet Offensive on the Pusan Perimeter. If you don't recognize those references, Google them and you'll see what I mean.

John was stationed in Okinawa, then, for complicated circumstances and one bad decision, in Vietnam. We corresponded, but it was cumbersome. Our letters would travel to an Army Post Office (APO) in San Francisco, them make their way back to Asia. I wrote more often than John did, but I knew that he had a fiancée, parents, and an older brother in the US who needed the reassurance of his well being more urgently than I. For my part, I was in less physical danger in Korea than I had been in college in Washington, D.C., and I had ample leisure time. Besides, he and I would have a lifetime of friendship when we rotated back to the States and were discharged.

Back in the US in August, 1968, I—a civilian—was immersed in job-hunting while my fiancée and future mother-in-law planned our wedding for October 12. In Washington to interview with the C.I.A., I connected with the friend who had given me the heads-up about John; he was then a third-year student at Georgetown medical school. Talking on a sidewalk in Georgetown, he told me of a classmate of ours who had been killed in Vietnam. I remembered him as a nice fellow and real gentle soul, to the point where I had trouble picturing him in the Army, let alone in combat.

Then, my friend said, "Oh, you know who else was killed in Vietnam...what was that guy's name?"

"Not John Coll."

"Yes. Oh, I forgot. Did you ever wind up meeting him?"

In an instant, I passed from naiveté through sorrow to awareness.

When we reported for our first duty station at Aberdeen Proving Grounds in Maryland, most of my comrades shared two assumptions with me: one, we were going to Vietnam, and two, we would not be killed there. Between us, John and I burst both assumptions.

Over the years, no more than several days have passed without John's coming to mind. He pops into my consciousness if I'm reading or watching television about our troops in Afghanistan or Iraq, or if I come across a former soldier's memories of a past war, Vietnam or others. Often, John appears with no prompt I am aware of.

I often think of John when I am encountering one of the challenges of life, thinking to myself, "John, if you were here, you'd help me figure this out." Because John missed out not only on the joys of marriage, children, friendships, but also the struggle of making a living and making a life—the main stuff of our time on earth.

Memorial Day, 2019

Part 12

AGING

AGING

Katherine Marotta

Give me a break, if you will...please
I am awake
To do all that I intend to do

Although I am gray
I still manage my way
To do all that I intend to do

When I was young,
Life seemed fun, fun, fun
I did all that I intended to do

In youth time seemed forever
I never said never
And I did all, yes all, that I wanted to do

It seems today, awake still
I still have the will
I slowly stopped expecting to do all
I want and intend to do

It seems that I must
Depend on my trust
And be at peace with all that I can do

WISDOM'S CHOICE
Wendy Bradford

Old Man: Fountain, What say you?

Fountain: Old Man, I say, you can be young again!

Old Man: Yes, but you require payment.

Fountain: Naturally, nothing is gratis.

Old Man: Then what is the cost?

Fountain: The cost is not great. It's just your knowledge.

Old Man: My knowledge, how can you be so irreverent? It's necessary to my life. It is my life.

Fountain: You give it too much measure. Youth is much better. Beauty prefers youth. Youth is magnetic for all. Youth can jump and run far better than you. Youth has no aches and pains.

Old Man: This is very true, yet not very deep.

Fountain: Deep, I don't understand. I am very deep.

Old Man: I mean to say profound. I suffer from many aches and pains. Yes, I would enjoy the vigor of my former self. Yet, through the years, I welcomed more the intellect than the physical.

Fountain: I thought I was offering you a gift.

Old Man: No gift should ever steal from me what is mine.

Fountain: Truly puzzling. Then, you would not pick any age to which you would gladly go back and relive?

Old Man: I have pondered on this and concluded NO. How can I relive something that you have taken from me as toll to the journey of my new life?

Fountain: Why?

Old Man: You speak in riddles. This is a circular argument of wasted time of learning and memories of family and friends. My knowledge and experiences of any age gone. Each age adding to the self that I am. A blank page, I would become. Who do you know would find interest in a book full of blank pages? No Fountain, the reckoning is too great for me. What then would my life mean to me if I lost my identity? You are a devil in disguise to promote this offer. I simply reject it.

Fountain: That's deep.

WHAT AGE WOULD YOU RECOVER IF YOU COULD MAGICALLY BECOME YOUNGER?
Wendy Bradford

What if you were offered to drink from the Fountain of Youth? You could become young again, but you would have to leave behind your life's learnings. Would you accept the offer?

So as I was pondering the idea of reverting to a younger self and to what age I would go back to, I thought why not? Of course, if I knew what I know now, I could have a good chance of making a better me. Oh but that's the hitch. What we have learned is not included in this "Youth Package." We literally have to start the learning process again.

When you take away the knowledge that you have accumulated throughout your life, you now start with a blank canvas. The portrait that was you is gone. A person is painted by the tools used to connect him to the human experience.

If you revert to your teens, or your twenties, or a bit older, on what do you build a foundation to make the new you? Any of these ages could be inappropriate as you would have created child-like and disadvantaged adults. What we commonly call people as "intellectually and developmentally disabled." (Other terms are "cognitive disability" or "challenged.") Clearly, not a condition most would choose to start their life over with.

In the opposite direction, dementia is feared much like cancer was a decade ago. Without your memories, what are you? It is why we sympathize so much with those who are affected by or caring for an individual, suffering from memory disorders or disease. We automatically feel the loss that someone feels, who becomes bereft of his or her memories. We put ourselves in their place sharing their sense of loss.

My preference would be to revert back to a newborn to avoid a more challenged life. Yet some think that we would just repeat what we had done in our first life. So then, why would we do it again if there is no improvement? Letting the Fountain of Youth talk you into becoming young again with no wisdom from your previous life is just plain foolish. Forget about it!

.

Part 13

HEALING

A true story with fictional embellishments

BRINGING HOME THE FLAG

Hugh M. Ryan

On the penultimate day of US Army R.O.T.C. summer training, August, 1965, my company commander, Captain John Pipkin, called me into his office, handed me the American flag our battalion had been flying, and told me to bury it in the woods.

"Bury it, sir?" I asked.

"Yes, that's the simplest prescribed way to dispose of an American flag."

"I realize that sir, but six weeks ago, this flag was brand new and it still looks hardly used. It seems a waste to discard it. Rather than burying it, may I keep it?"

"No, it's government property, and I have no authority to transfer ownership to you."

"Then, may I take it back to the R.O.T.C. unit at Georgetown?"

"Is there a shortage of flags in the nation's capital that I'm not aware of?"

"No sir, not to my knowledge."

"This battalion will no longer exist as of 14:00 hours tomorrow. The filling out the paperwork to transfer ownership from this battalion to Georgetown would keep you and me here until next summer. Just take the flag to the woods and bury it. You seem like a reasonably bright guy, so I assume you understand my order. If you don't agree with it, I really don't care."

"Sir, may I ask a question?"

"If you must."

"Are you going to dispatch someone to accompany me into the woods to ensure that I really bury the flag?"

"No."

"When we depart tomorrow, is anyone going to inspect our luggage to ensure we have no contraband?"

"No."

I saluted and took the flag to the supply sergeant's office where I signed out a shovel, telling the sergeant my purpose, to maintain my cover story.

"I don't care why you want the shovel," the sergeant said. "I care only that you bring it back. If you don't, you're paying for it."

Off to the supposed burial grounds, flag and shovel in hand. I walked into the woods where no one could see me, stuffed the flag inside my shirt, dirtied the shovel blade, and returned to the supply sergeant.

"I hope you don't think you're going to turn a dirty shovel in to me," he said.

I explained in detail how and why I had soiled his shovel, maintaining the cover story to conceal my theft of government property.

"You seem to think that I care about your activities," the supply sergeant said. "I don't. I just want my shovel back, clean. Or you're paying for it."

After satisfying the supply sergeant's order, I went to my bunk and, when no one was looking, secreted the flag in my suitcase.

My father, a naturalized American citizen who served as a commissioned officer in the United States Army during World War II, loved all the iterations of the American flag, dating to the 13-star Betsy Ross version, and flew a flag at our house every day, weather-permitting.

At home, I unpacked the flag, found my father outside, and said, "I have something for you, dad."

"What's that, old boy?"

"This is the flag that flew over our battalion."

He looked as though I'd just given him a chest of krugerrands, and immediately replaced the flag he'd been flying. That flag joined his collection, and flew now and then, with the others, until he aged to the point where he could no longer indulge himself in this custom.

When he died in 1995, I finally obeyed Captain Pipkin's order, burying with my father the flag for which he had held an immigrant citizen's reverence.

ASYLUM HAVEN
Katherine Marotta

In December we visit a cement building miles away from the center of the small city of Vitoria da Conquista, Brazil. It is considered an Asylum, named *Abrigo Nosso Lar*, "Our Home Shelter." One sees the electric wires on the top of the walls and the entry gate is locked. This is the way it is. Private homes are secured in the same manner. We ring the bell and are greeted with a warm, *Bem-vindo*, "Welcome."

It houses people from the street—the poor, elderly, mentally, and physically challenged. Today they all wait for us inside with excited expectation. Every Christmas season my husband's family, led by his sister Mercia, goes to a special holiday event here.

The wheelchairs are occupied by at least five waiting residents sitting inches apart from thirty or more comfortably occupied chairs. There are two or three residents strolling around on foot. My first facility tour three years ago need not be revisited. All is stable. Shared private rooms house two roommates. Some beds have little dolls resting there. The activity room displays shelves of colorful hand-made crafts. The showers, the hospital-like infirmary, the kitchen with busy cooks preparing meals, are immaculately clean. Nothing smells except the food in the kitchen. It appears sparse yet spacious with hand railed areas for outside garden strolls.

We observe two residents being fed with a spoon, both sipping from their sippy cups. What strikes the visitor is the peacefulness as staff moves from place to person always assisting with soft voices. Everyone seems to know exactly what needs to be done.

If the visitor wants to socialize they can meet extended hands for a shake or embrace two eagerly extended arms for a hug. If you have a seat you may get touched, hear compliments, or a repeated phrase. Some folks respond, some don't.

Our nephew João Carlos brings his three-year-old son. The residents are introduced to João Miguel as *avo'* and *avó*, grandma and grandpa. João Miguel has no hesitancy and gladly says, *Ola*, "Hello" while curiously eyeing the piles of gifts. The ladies consistently say *bonzinho, bonitinho*, "good little boy" and "little cutey" and want to touch him. He's fine with it.

Today we are met by the good looking older gentleman resident Senhor Luis. We've seen him every year. As is his style, everyday he wears his dress shirt and tie and hat. My husband chats, shakes his hand, and pats his back with a left arm hug. The smile and nodding goes on as Senhor Luis reports that he is still well and happy.

The band enters, assembles directly in front of the audience, and the festivities begin. The local police band in full beige uniform with their brass and drums offer Christmas carols. Folks clap and the sound of voices escalate. Focused on the music, there is rocking and laughing, and some cover their ears. We sing.

Each name is called and each visitor presents an elaborately wrapped gift to one individual, as we say *Feliz Natal*. We assist if they choose to open them. Most do but some want to wait and just keep touching and admiring their gift. If they were able, they previously asked for something specific, like a hat, flip-flops, a new doll, a blouse, a shirt, or perfume. One can't help but remember that feeling when receiving an anticipated gift.

Not all the receivers have that memory, but the immediate joy, most do. Senhor Luis had asked for and received a wristwatch. He is elated adding to his elegance. We know he must have been, and perhaps still is a ladies man.

After the gifts are given we all get to eat the now revealed goodies presented on the tables. Cakes, cheese, and coconut breads, chicken all prepared Brazilian style. Generosity, kindness, and appreciation are the themes for the day.

The bathing, feeding, medicating, and general care is done by volunteers. The funding is generated from the community, doctors, businesses, all organized and operated by members of a spiritualist group. My sister-in-law, Mercia, is a Spiritualist and a fundraiser. Spiritualists believe in an afterlife.

Mercia's pride is apparent as she flits around from staff to visitors to residents. I find the experience humbling, often brought to tears, as I struggle with the reality of the situation.

These fragile residents have no families, no money, and limited memories. They are at their life's end, barely speak, few can walk, yet the visitor can see a sparkle in their eyes. The dedication and care given so freely to others is heroic. I call these heroes angels. This asylum called, "Our Home Shelter" offers a safe human haven, and perhaps a little bit of sweet heaven here on Mother Earth.

TRAVELERS
Wendy Bradford

Leaning against a tree off the road
Disappointment was his name.
Anger, his sister, was already at my side,
having traveled with me for a week.

As a lover, Loneliness, had joined me before.
So desperate for companionship,
I was lured by his deceitful attentions.
"Go there, Go anywhere, Go where?"

Over paths and mounds,
these combined burdens rode with us.
Our tracks crooked and haphazard
and me and my horse misguided.

For my nearsighted thoughts
had greatly weighed upon my truest friend
To the blacksmith we limped to remove
the offending pebbles birthed by sorrow.

Strange the force they held on me.
I could not let go of these stones
in my satchel against my heart
I carried them much like a false badge of honor.

Knowing I could no longer voyage so,
I stopped by the pond of despair.
skipping the stones out to the surface rippling,
A furious sense of freedom shook my soul.

Today, I picked up a new hitchhiker.
Regrets was no burden.

as he lightened our journey with knowledge
and a clear sight with new purpose.

Disappointment had left me out of control
of circumstances not my making.
Regrets left me understanding that control
came from wiser decisions.

DUKE
Mel Jolly

We don't know where he came from. He just showed up one day, begging for food. Like other dogs in our neighborhood, he was a mixture, only no one could identify just what that mixture was. Anyway, this dog we called Duke was pretty unusual in many ways. Oh, he did all the usual tricks of begging for food, scratching on the door to be let out, and even sleeping at the foot of my bed every night.

But Duke was not only smart, he was clever as well. He seemed to understand humans better than most humans. If you were sad or feeling low, he instinctively would come over next to you and try to cheer you up by doing backward flips or walking on his hind legs. When he finished his tricks, he would sit down in front of you and look up as if to say, "Are you feeling better now?" You couldn't help but smile at him, give him a hug, or shake his paw.

Duke was our own personal carrier pigeon. He brought the newspaper in every day, and often he also brought in the mail when it was delivered by the postman. But I think Duke's best trait of all was his awareness of people approaching our house. As soon as someone began to come up the walkway toward the house, Duke announced the impending arrival by tapping your leg two or three times. If it was a stranger who was about to arrive, the tapping would be accompanied by a low growl, but if it was a family member or friend, just the leg tapping was enough—no growl needed. This consistent procedure usually baffled our guests, who generally were totally surprised to see the door opening before they even rang the doorbell.

Duke liked children, so we frequently took him to visit the children's ward at the hospital, the local orphanage, and other youth facilities. As kids are prone to do, they often pulled Duke's tail, patted him too hard, or whistled too loudly around him, but Duke was such a trooper he never became in the slightest bit aggressive.

One day a stranger came to the house and inquired whether we had seen a dog that fit Duke's description. My mother, not being one to tell stories, admitted a dog meeting that description had become her son's pet. The stranger explained to Mom that he was from the circus, which had recently been in town, and the dog was a circus performer. As a matter of fact, the stranger said the dog's real name was Stanley, and he actually was the star of the circus. Somehow Stanley had gotten loose, and everyone thought he was dead, until the circus members began hearing about a dog who had been entertaining children at various facilities in the area. On a chance, the stranger from the circus was investigating if perhaps that dog was in fact Stanley.

I was on my way home from school the day the stranger was talking with my Mother, and as usual, Duke met me halfway to the house, and we walked the rest of the way together. When we arrived at home, we went in the back door and I started to get Duke something to eat, but he began to growl. I looked around behind him just in time to see a strange man standing by the front door talking with my Mother. Mom explained to me who he was and why he was at the house. I felt as though I had been run over by a truck, numb from head to toe, speechless, and afraid. Duke watched me and then came over to pat my leg two or three times.

The stranger told me his story and that my Duke was really Stanley, who belonged with the circus. He proceeded to put Duke/Stanley on a leash and was starting to leave when Duke/Stanley stopped in his tracks. Try as he might, the stranger could not get Duke/Stanley to move from that spot. Finally, he took off the leash, and without a moment's hesitation, Duke/Stanley ran back to me and licked my face, his tail furiously wagging. The stranger watched how overjoyed Duke/Stanley was, and finally nodded his head, gave me a hand salute, and started to walk away.

Duke and I ran after the stranger, but when we tried to thank him, the man stopped and turned around to face me. Then he told me, "Son, a good dog can change a day, a great dog can change a life. Remember that you have a great dog and treat him as he deserves to be treated every day. Do I have your word on that?"

As the stranger turned to walk away again, I said, "Yes, Sir, you do." Duke and I stood there and watched the stranger as he disappeared into the distance—the stranger who gifted new lives to both Duke and me. Only later did I learn that stranger was Mr. P.T. Barnum.

THE SAVOY
Al Clemence

It was a cold day in March. A blustery wind was chasing the remnants of winter along the streets of the city. A late winter walk on a cold but sunny morning that had offered relief from the monotony of domestic confinement had withdrawn that promise. Now as I tugged my cap to secure it over numb ears, I looked for shelter from the mischievous wind. I turned a corner at the end of the street aided by the forceful encouragement of a strong gust. As I recovered my balance, the welcoming sign of the Savoy Hotel was directly before me. The lobby had been recently restored and now offered a small coffee bar as a companion to an ample reading area and bookstore. It would be the perfect destination for my ambulatory misadventure.

As the door closed behind me, the aroma of freshly brewed coffee became the ambassador of a welcomed greeting. With a warm cup securely in my hand, I wandered along the rows of books toward the sitting area, where two large windows separated the wind from the light that defined the scene outside. Beyond an ancient river, whose gentle current still carries the name given by Native Americans, the land rose sharply to create a path. Steel rails drawn with parallel precision defined the course to destinations beyond the horizon.

Sheltered here between the rows of books that chronicle adventures completed and facing the path to adventures that have yet to be imagined, I relaxed to enjoy a moment in time.

SAFE HARBOR
Wendy Bradford

Such a beautiful day, the hull sliced through the water as the sun danced upon it, repeating the rippling over the bay. We had come in second among the twenty-three boats racing and Dad gleamed with pride. His young crew had performed well. Now, Mom began to relax as we moved towards our final destination of the day. Here, we would anchor together and sit down to hors d'oeuvres, drinks, dinner, and no precarious surfaces or excitement.

In a minute, the sky turned a gunmetal gray and the cold kiss of the wind smacked my cheek. Rain pelted down on my t-shirt and the temperature nosedived. I received an immediate shower of salty water dunking me with no warning of the microburst storm we were to experience.

The waves curled into rising crescents over father's head as he grasped the tiller, erratically swinging him from side to side. My brother, Tom, who a minute earlier tried to bring down the jib, was hanging from it. Each time the wind assaulted the jib, it expanded the growing hole in the sail. Tom's body rocketed up and down ten or more feet as he held on to it. At the same time, the boat's bow bent down to the sea like a drunken sailor's exaggerated bow to a woman he would impress.

With bungee cords in my mouth and clinging to the boom, I slapped at the mainsail to tie it down. No time for neatness. A cold realization came that a monster had descended on us, we, its victims. Too many boats were zipping about in a cove much too small for this chaos.

The mainsail tied. I turned to help Tom. His violent elevator rides on the jib were threatening to fling him out into the water. There are those times when you feel on the precipice of choice and direction. At fifteen, I steadied myself as I studied my choices. Hugging the cabin, I felt myself trip and surf past the boat's edge, only to feel the iron fist of my four foot, ten inch, 120-pound mother wrap itself around my ankle.

I yelled to Dad. "What do I do?" No answer returned. The roar of the wind dominated all sound.

Be brave, you are going to have to figure this out and quickly. Do what you can, I thought.

So I continued the crawl to the bow to help my brother tame that son of a bitch jib. When done, we returned to the mainsail to find that it had continued to tear itself, whipping against the steel stays holding the mast up. Could we stop something worse from happening? Sometimes that is all you can do.

So preoccupied with battling our own sails, I didn't notice the many near misses my father and the other boat captains prevented. Boats were scraping by us from all sides. I looked up to see the intensely blue eyes of Yardley "Yardbird" Smith staring us down as we seemed to torpedo towards the middle of his beautiful mahogany sixty-five-foot sloop. Dad waved us all to the stern and increased the motor speed as he missed the Smiths by a hair's breathe.

The finality of the storm was as quick as its birth. As we motored back to the nearest port to take refuge, we saw many boats with damaged sails, a few had lost their masts, one boat lay against a jetty beach, another on the rocks, and a small roof floated by us.

Magnificent sunset ribbons exploded in the sky. It was then my mother brought up four metallic shot cups with finger high portions of Dutch gin. She looked at us saying "Thank you."

Battle weary, each of us had done their part. The expert had had faith in his crew despite its amateur status. He was now proud and thankful for the best reason—a safe return.

The following day, two new sails were ordered, a steering wheel would replace the tiller, and my mother had insisted on a call radio. We would live another day for another storm.

KATHY AGE 5ISH
Katherine Marotta

They called her Kathy then
Her name it was not
She had no control, no choice
A lifetime that name hated, never forgot
Now she uses her name that at birth was given
Her mother picked that simple nickname
As a child, Kathy had to listen
Especially because her mother's name was the same
Kathy was taken to the circus
Brother too, a three ring
Barnum and Bailey, a freak show included
For Kathy age 5ish it all had a sting
Climbing the bleachers
Was frightening and scary
Taking steps slowly
Alone, with each step little Kathy was wary
Older brother loved the climb up
Went quickly, his first time too
Kathy, feeling so nervous and cautious
Something she did not want to do
But finally up they all went
The family to see performances so high
Three rings of movement
As the trapeze did fly
Kathy's attention was distracted
During the show and its features
Instead she noticed another girl climbing
Like her, also frightened, climbing the bleachers
A girl, but large, not young, wearing a red coat and tam
Was offered care, slowly guided to her seat
Someone so gently held her hand
Kathy starred and wanted the girl's eyes to meet

It was explained the red coated girl was special
And one must not stare
Look at the clowns and elephants
Of that be aware

Attention to the circus was not so important
Kathy felt something very profound just happened for sure
Her little girl self felt a life message was sent
Knowing she herself was missing care and wanted more
Years passed and each time Kathy needed comfort
Suffering, Kathy would cry
And prayed and wished she was special like the circus girl
It must be better that way...but she wondered why
Kathy grew longing for the comfort of love
Purposely moving through life as one should
Never forgetting the day of her lesson
A brief moment of time teaching her that loving was good

Excerpt from "Every Day is Sun Day"

ESCAPING MY MORTAL COIL
Cynthia F. Davidson

Despite the inauspicious set up, what occurred that week did the most to change the course of my life when the turning points are seen in retrospect. The initial plan had been to spend that time with someone else, but when he was called away at the last minute, I did not cancel the arrangements. Instead they turned into an unexpected *rendezvous* with my Self. How rarely we make appointments to be with ourselves. We rush to make room for others in our lives with scant regard for what we might be missing when we do.

Providentially, my ticket was already purchased and the hotel reserved, so I departed from my trying work life in London, to spend that week alone in Lebanon. Arriving at the Beirut hotel, I checked into one of its anonymous rooms on the fifth floor. Before unpacking, I opened the one window that faced east and breathed deeply. The scent of the Mediterranean Sea, crashing upon the rocks a few blocks to the west, reached this far and soothed me.

For the next five days I did not leave the room. The spiritual suggestion of fasting had been incubating for a long time, initially seeded by Sunday school instructions, like the forty days and forty nights story of Jesus in the Judean desert. Like the wise ones, I wanted to plumb the depths. Rather than rely upon what they had discovered, I wanted to find out the truth for myself. To explore what lay beyond, get to the bottom or over the top of what troubled me at the tender age of twenty. Believing this was a way to seek guidance and request directions from whatever powers exist in the Universe, I wanted to strip away everything else that distracted from pure knowing.

I did not call room service and had no food or drinks with me. Occasionally I brewed mint tea on the tiny hot plate. I sat, I slept, I sipped, and I dreamed. So many thoughts traveled through me, coming and going, including images of floating in the bathtub, a jeweled necklace of opal stones around my neck....

On the afternoon of the fifth day, while reclining upon the bedcovers with my hands folded over my belly, the separation happened. I was suddenly outside my body. Having never heard the term "out of body experience," I was unprepared for this. But being able to look down, upon the dozing "me" from up above, was amazing. Elation filled me. I could feel the left hand corner of the ceiling pressing against whatever was still me, and adjusted to this brand new awareness, of being free. This remaining part of conscious me could pass through these walls, fly anywhere, totally unencumbered—exhilaration did little to describe these sensations.

But just as quickly, fear zoomed back in to distract me. The fright of the unknown, of not knowing how to get back inside my body, and the "I" dying as a result, instantly reunited me with my human overcoat. I reasoned I was "playing" with a much larger realm, more powerful than I was ready for. Unschooled and without a proper teacher, I needed to put these things away until it was the right time. Sitting up, shaken, but relieved I went downstairs for my first meal.

The wait to resume fasting and these mystical studies lasted two decades.

Part 14

ENDINGS

COLORS

Song Lyrics by Cynthia F. Davidson

A green woman holds a heart in her hand
A blue one holds a tear
A brown woman stays so close to the land
A red one's warm and near.
A yellow sleeps in the meadow grass
A black one comes undone
A gray woman holds a looking glass
And so the rainbow ladies pass.
And so the rainbow ladies pass.

STARLIGHT AT THE END OF THE DAY
Al Clemence

I stand alone on a clear, cold night, stars seem to surround me like snowflakes in a late winter squall.

The night sky belongs to me; yet, I cannot protect it from the dawn.

What will protect us from the battles that are sure to come?

What could replace the sparkle that now fills the night?

Will there still be time to find our way, when we can no longer see the nearest shore?

When we wander in darkness through tunnels carved in the black remains of species long extinct, how much, then, would we freely share for starlight at the end of day?

ACKNOWLEDGMENTS

We, the Westerly Library's Adult Writing Group, have formed a group to provide an intelligent, respectful, and supportive space for those who wish to practice the art of writing. We enjoy workshops on members' ongoing works in progress, discussions on topics, which include guest speakers or writing topics, and regular prompts for the members to write essay, fiction, or poetry. We wish to support this community, this library, and our members.

We extend our deepest gratitude to Erik Caswell for forming this group and guiding it intelligently and creatively. He has provided us a foundation worth building on.

Our mission in this anthology is to provide our members the rewarding opportunity of seeing their work in print.

All essays, fictional or true, and poetic pieces represent a universal theme of Journey: the act of traveling from one place to another in a physical or spiritual way.

Other acknowledgments are:

Editor and book design: Gigie Hall
Front Photo: Marcos Andrade

Contributing Members
Barstow, Jane
Bradford, Wendy
Caswell, Erik
Capizzano, Stephen
Clemence, Al
Davidson, Cynthia
Huang, Phoebe
Jolly, Mel
Leigh, Katharine
Marotta, Katherine
Maynard, Eric
Rosenzweig, Andy
Ryan, Hugh
Weiss, Emma

ABOUT THE WESTERLY WRITING GROUP

On January 6, the first snowy Saturday morning of 2018, seven strangers pulled off our coats and pulled up our chairs around a large wooden table in an upstairs reference room of the Westerly Public Library. Not knowing what to expect, we had all sorts of reasons for showing up at this brand new adult writing group and some were yet to be discovered.

Our facilitator was Erik Caswell, a young assistant librarian who I had crossed paths with the previous autumn at a University of Rhode Island Writers conference. Both of us were renewing our commitments to our solitary craft, but neither of us wanted to go it alone, and we knew others who had expressed an interest in the same goals. A few of us had tried before and failed to find the type of community we sought, yet here we were determined to try again.

Almost two years later, as we approach the end of 2019, we realize we have done it. Together we've created what we needed and this anthology is proof that our writing can outlive us. What a journey of trial and error it has been.

At the start, we met every other Saturday as people of every stripe came and went. Younger. Older. Experienced and novice scribblers. Some only came when summering in Rhode Island, so they drifted off·to winter elsewhere, although our email list continued to expand. Many who showed up were shy, having lacked the time to practice writing, or the belief they had it in them. We admired their attempts to try again because we had faced the same demons.

Somewhere sits a fat three ring binder full of the pages we produced during our group's inception. Early on, someone suggested weekly prompts, so we rotated the duty to come up with them. Our fearless facilitator kindly printed out our emailed compositions, 500 words at a go. Occasionally we wrote on the spot, with five minutes to pen whatever came to mind about a word like storm, or petty, hypocrisy, and loathsome.

Figuring out how to get the words down is one thing. Finding out how they resonate with readers is another magnitude of challenge. Live readings with real people require courage. We discovered more was expected from us—in a good way—and we learned to give and receive feedback that encouraged each other when the mark was missed, and even how to accept praise when we hit it.

Becoming more articulate readers galvanized our efforts to become better writers. We were soon meeting every Saturday from 10:30 to noon. Our regular exchanges compounded our energies, growing both the trust and the inspiration necessary to bridge the gaps between how our words landed when we read them aloud, and what they actually meant to others.

Eventually we outgrew our original space and moved downstairs to a larger ground floor glass room. And Erik moved on to a better job just across the state line, but he left us well established. He set us up on Google, where we track our multiple scheduled offerings and managed sign-ups as our membership increased. Now we can workshop up to five pages from our own projects, or volunteer to facilitate sessions on favorite writers or genres we're familiar with, like police procedurals or Westerns. Sometimes visitors come to share their books with us and we even hosted a panel of local authors.

That old adage about the journey being more important than the destination has proven true for our evolving Westerly writing group and this writing journey has reaffirmed our faith in the power of sharing stories and poetry. The benefits continue to surprise us. To be heard, understood, and appreciated by each other is such a gift.

— Cynthia F. Davidson

To learn more about our Westerly Writers group,
come in person any Saturday, from 10:30 to noon or visit:
bit.ly/WesterlyGroup

For questions or more information, please contact Marilyn Russo at:
mrusso@westerlylibrary.org

Westerly Library
44 Broad St.
Westerly, RI 02891
United States